BOY, INTERRUPTED

THE MURDER OF GANNON STAUCH

By Nick van der Leek

"My son burned the carpet, how do I fix it?"
— Letecia Stauch Google Search on January 27th,
the day Gannon Stauch disappeared

Important Note to the Reader:

The Rocket Science books are unique. Throughout this book, the author has provided hyperlinks to relevant resources including documents, photographs and videos to enhance your interactivity with the story.

Disclaimer

At the time of writing, <u>THE PEOPLE OF THE STATE OF COLORADO vs. LETECIA STAUCH</u> is a pending murder trial. Letecia Stauch currently faces 13 charges including murder in the first degree, with intent and after deliberation, child abuse resulting in death, tampering with a deceased human body, tampering with physical evidence, and other counts including crimes of violence. This narrative follows the prosecution's case based on an interpretation and analysis of the 32-page Stauch Affidavit. According to point 194 on page 32 of the affidavit's concluding remarks, Letecia Stauch was indisputably the last known person to see Gannon Stauch before his death and disappearance.

Table Of Contents

Monday Murder

"I was a naughty kid." — Liam Hemsworth

Far above a row of almost new houses lining Mandan Drive in Colorado Springs, the silver prairie moon slips down through broken clouds, and out of sight. The last dog finishes up barking. <u>Hollering human voices</u> agitate before settling down again. For some it's a relief that the next day is a school day. For others, like eleven-year-old Gannon Stauch, there's one last chance to play.

One by one golden squares all along the drive go out. By midnight an icy gloom, black as pitch, settles over the buttoned-down neighborhood. Various devices programmed to keep time quietly record Sunday, January 26th becoming Monday the 27th. This midwinter Monday starts like every other day – in darkness. But then something stirs. Inside one house on Mandan Drive, a 36-year-old woman with raven-black hair taps her index finger against the bright square of her iPhone:

my son.burned the carpet how.do I fix.it

It's exactly nine-and-a-half minutes after midnight. The illuminated iPhone is reduced to two tiny squares in Letecia Stauch's black eyes. For a long time Gannon's stepmother, who has some training as a teaching assistant, types in various search terms.

00:42:50 *will humidifier.help.if.exposed to smoke*[1]

00:43:20 *smoke affects will humidifier help*

00:43:30 *smoke from fire will humidifier help*

It's not clear whether Letecia has been sickened by the smoke, or Gannon. Since Gannon had undisclosed health problems, it's possible smoke inhalation from burning the carpet the previous night, along with Letecia's emotional hysteria, aggravated his condition. Regardless of health issues, whatever went up in smoke inside the house aggravated some kill switch in Gannon's stepmother. Twelve minutes after the trifecta of smoke/humidifier searches, Letecia's search takes on a different tone, and intent. Letecia's index finger taps compulsively against the bright square of her iPhone:

00:55:40 *colorado law for kid staying at home*

00:57:20 *School is out. Is it okay for my kid to stay home alone?*

01:01:25 *son is sick but I have to.go to.work*

01:03:25 *son sick can he stay.home*

The quaint house with its American flag out front reeks of smoke, and swelling disquiet. Gannon is ill [or upset] and can't sleep. Letecia is stuck babysitting her stepchild, and evidently going to be stuck with him all night and all through Monday as well. Where's Al? As usual he's no help. <u>Al's a Current Operations Officer</u> with the 100th Missile Defense Brigade. Like many wives of military men, Letecia's facing another long weekend with her husband away again, this time in Oklahoma or Dallas. He left Saturday from Denver International. He'll be back Tuesday, flying into Colorado Springs Airport.

---

1 When investigators arrived at the Stauch home late on the night January 27th, they didn't smell any smoke. According to page 20 of the <u>Stauch Affidavit</u>: *There was no odor of smoke, and no evidence of smoke…One Detective noted the basement smelled like coconut, and was very pleasant.*

After an hour of exasperated online searching, Letecia searches for online succor on social media. But neither Facebook nor the images on Instagram are able to lift Letecia's spirits. At some point she also lets Al know that Gannon's not going to school:

"I'm just going to give them an excuse at work and stay with him..."

Unsatisfied, and at the end of another miserable weekend, Letecia drifts off in and out of a restless sleep. Does Gannon need care and attention through the night as well? Three hours and forty minutes after her last online search, Letecia reaches for her phone again.

Letecia texts her employer at **04:37** that her stepdad's been killed after being hit by a car. She's not going to be coming into work that day. She also texts Grand Mountain Elementary, Gannon's school, who will mark him as absent and excused that day.

She's right about one thing: someone not directly related to her *is* going to die violently that day, at her hands, and because of that, she won't be at work. Three minutes later we see what else is uppermost on Letecia's mind.

04:40:40 *suede repair kit for sofa*

In the early hours, as the winter sun propped itself over the rim of the prairie in the east, painting the snow-capped tips of the Rockies gold, Letecia set about getting her other stepchild, Laina [eight] and Harley [her biological daughter, 17] ready for the day. At **08:13,** possibly once Harley and Laina had left, **Letecia snapped an image of Gannon asleep in his bed.** Four minutes later, at **08:17,** Letecia snapped a second image. The point of these photos may have been to be able to send to Al, or to show whoever asked where Gannon was that morning, or how he was that morning. It's also possible, though not necessarily likely, if Letecia had formed a murderous intent by this point, that she wanted the images so she could recreate the scene after Gannon was gone.

In these images from Monday morning Gannon's Nintendo Switch is visible right beside him, on the bed.

Almost two hours later, at **09:56**, and just fifteen minutes prior to running an errand that morning [that went on until the afternoon], Letecia does something that's very unlike her. Letecia's a heavy smartphone and social media user. It's the start of the day, the beginning of another work week, but she *locks her phone.*

At **10:16**, Gannon and Letecia get into a red Nissan Frontier, and drive off. In an ominous and portentous parallel to the Watts case, the Frontier is parked on the road in front of the driveway, and Letecia gets in, backs it up the driveway to the garage, before driving off in the direction of neighbor Roderrick Drayton's surveillance camera. Although the moment of Letecia and Gannon's departure is captured on <u>Drayton's security camera</u>, the footage from several houses away is grainy and unclear. 21 minutes after leaving home a message is dispatched from Gannon's phone to Harley, Letecia's teenage daughter.

10:37 *Tecia left phone at home if you need her text me.*

Did Gannon send this message at his stepmother's instruction, or did Letecia simply take Gannon's phone [she would soon acquire permanent custody of the crucial device] and begin leaving digital breadcrumbs?

Purchase receipts and CCTV footage prove where the boy and his stepmother went to next. Petco is just 22 miles from the Stauch home. Letecia was seen in the area at **11:22**. It took Letecia about twice as long to drive there compared to the timing provided by Google Maps. Gannon isn't visible during this visit to Petco.

At **12:06**, Al Stauch sends his son a text: *Hey Buddy.* But Gannon doesn't answer. When Letecia makes her second appearance at Petco at **13:22** on North Nevada Avenue, Gannon still isn't visible. Around the same time, at **13:21**, Gannon's phone responds to Al's text. Gannon's request to his father is about his Nintendo.

Can I play Zelda at least

If this message is from Gannon, it's communicating 1) that he's not being allowed to do something and 2) that he's asking for an exception on a possible gaming embargo. Clearly a kid not being allowed to do something he wants to do within the context of that child's murder, potentially shows the operative dynamics.

On the other hand, Letecia may have sent the message to seed the psychology that Gannon wanted to play a game, wasn't allowed to and thus had reason to run away from home [which was Letecia's original bogus story]. Al's response to this request apparently from his 11-year-old son is curt:

Not today.

One can imagine Gannon not responding very well to this news. Which 11-year-old would? Stuck home, sick, stuck with a disapproving stepmom, in trouble because of the fire and basically grounded.

At **13:43** the affidavit describes "a significant event" occurring about half-an-hour before Gannon and Letecia arrived back from their errand. Gannon's phone made the following online search:

can my parent find my cell phone.if its off

Law enforcement suspects Letecia sent this text and yes, she likely did. Why though? It's not clear whether Letecia herself wanted to know the information, but it seems plausible she did. She needed to know the status of Gannon's phone right then, didn't she? Having already decided to murder Gannon, Letecia wanted to know about practical things like what to do with his phone. Should she dispose of it with him, or was that likely to assist the cops in finding the body [through the phone]?[2] Clearly, this was the central dilemma faced by Chris Watts. Bear in mind, at that very moment Letecia's phone was at home so she knew *her* movements couldn't be traced. The same psychology applies to Gannon's phone. Whatever Letecia decides to do with Gannon's phone, the intention is to make sure Gannon isn't traceable. The premeditated aspect is playing out right here.

The Stauch Affidavit points out on page 5 that uncertainty exists regarding Letecia's movements with Gannon between 11:22 and 13:22. It's also unclear exactly where she was during what should have been a half-hour trip to Petco, when it took Letecia close to 66 minutes to complete the same journey. It's conceivable that Gannon's stepmother intended killing him that morning, perhaps even using the red vehicle to drive over him, but couldn't find a safe enough or secluded spot in broad daylight, and decided home was the better alternative.[3]

At **14:19** the Nissan Frontier returns to 6627 Mandan Drive. The vehicle has been AWOL for precisely four hours and three minutes. It stops, pauses in the road, then backs up the driveway between a tree and another vehicle [likely Letecia's black Volkswagen Tiguan].

The bulky red truck pulls forward, obviously having misjudged the angle, then backs up again, this time all the way up the driveway, partially obscuring the rear of the vehicle from neighbor Drayston's not quite all-seeing surveillance camera.[4]

---

2 Gannon's phone was found at home; a factor complicating the search for him but also a factor disproving he'd left voluntarily to visit a friend. Why do that without his phone?

3 If Letecia did head out with the intent to murder Gannon somewhere outside of the home, it would certainly explain the four hour period the two were away from home, as well as the apparently unusual activity visiting the same store twice on the same day.

4 Since no blood evidence was found in the Nissan Frontier, it appears the backing of the vehicle was intended as a false flag. If so, it worked. It's also

Although the thousands following this case on YouTube and social media held this grainy, fuzzy moment up as the strongest, incontrovertible, almost *conclusive* proof that Letecia had returned home without Gannon and thus proved there was foul play, proved Letecia murdered Gannon, law enforcement felt otherwise.

The Stauch Affidavit notes on page 5:

"After viewing the video, I cannot be sure if another person exited the vehicle or not, but I submit <u>Gannon likely did return home with Letecia that afternoon</u>…"

When Letecia arrived home with Gannon, despite the cell phone addict being without her phone for over four hours, she *still* didn't make a beeline for her phone. In fact, she didn't unlock her phone for another 25 minutes.[5]

Between **14:20** and **14:45** [when Letecia unlocked her phone], the ADT home security system recorded *a great deal of motion* upstairs and downstairs. Having returned from an arduous but unsuccessful scouting attempt for an appropriate killing and disposal site, and, finding the smell of burnt carpet still lingered in the house – *Gannon's doing* – Letecia finally had enough.

---

possible the Nissan Frontier was parked to block the view of the car on the opposite side – Letecia's Volkswagen Tiguan. Blood evidence was found in that vehicle.

5 Just as Shan'ann Watts behavior was out of character in terms of supposedly leaving her phone at home, Letecia's cell phone psychology is a character mismatch to her usual behavior.

Human Remains off Highway 90

"I've never been that cute kid that was forgiven for being naughty." — Richard C. Armitage

Sometime after 09:00 on March 16th, a Tuesday, a Florida Department of Transportation road crew are alerted to something <u>under a long bridge</u>. The terrain beside the <u>U.S. Route 90</u> highway is <u>rocky, downward sloping and treacherous</u>.

Upon closer inspection, the crew discover what appears to be the human remains of a boy.[6] The remains are <u>along the side of the bridge</u>, but <u>not in water</u>, nor in <u>the nearby Escambia River</u>.

Next a member from the Florida Department of Transportation road crew calls the Santa Rosa County Sheriff's Office in Florida. When the cops arrive they park on the left side of the highway nearest to the disposal site, and cordon off a sizable area with yellow bunting. A CSA tech <u>sets up a tripod and starts documenting and measuring the area</u>.

At the time of writing, it's unclear how the road construction workers were alerted to the human remains. Smell was probably the initial giveaway, followed – upon taking a closer look – by the sight of a brown suitcase not very carefully hidden.

---

6 It's uncertain whether the remains were found inside a suitcase, or whether the suitcase was open or nearby. There is some <u>consensus at the time of writing that the remains were associated, and probably transported, in a suitcase</u>.

The rock-strewn terrain adjacent to the highway makes it impossible to bury anything, so the only camouflage was either going lower down, out of line-of-sight under the bridge, or using the foliage for cover. Given the relatively close proximity of bushes to the highway, it seems logical to assume this would have been the easiest option, but clearly not the best option.

An area parallel to the crime scene tape but <u>on the opposite side of the highway</u> suggests a vehicle may have parked in the space just off the verge, where the verge ends and the bridge gradually starts. If the disposal occurred after dark, the perpetrator [unfamiliar with the area] may have assumed where the bridge started, so did the river. But while lugging the heavy suitcase over difficult, uneven, sloping rubble, <u>the perpetrator discovered the river wasn't close by at all</u>. Instead of returning to the vehicle with the suitcase, the perpetrator decided the area – though not perfect – was remote, hard to reach, unlikely for passers-by to reach, and so decided to make do with the disposal.

If the suitcase was dumped out of plain sight, it wasn't dumped far out of plain sight. The perpetrator may have reasoned the distance away from home made up for not putting in much of a physical effort from the roadside to the actual disposal site, and also didn't want to risk spending too much time struggling in the area, and raising suspicion.

If the visual range was sufficient to defeat a casual glance by passers-by, what about smell? The body was left well within the range of human smell for someone walking on the highway. The devious perpetrator hadn't factored that into the equation.

The boy's body is exposed and photographed, samples are taken, including samples from the fabric of the stained, putrid smelling suitcase. Insects and small organisms are carefully brushed aside. The deceased juvenile male is an advanced state of decomposition, immediately raising the question: *how long has it been here?*

Several long hours pass as more investigators and CSA techs are summoned to the scene. <u>Traffic needs to be redirected around it</u>. <u>Orange traffic cones are placed in the one lane</u> to provide the authorities with the space they need to study the scene. The tops of vehicles moving on the opposite side of the highway, crossing the Escambia from the Pensacola side, and heading towards Pace, try to catch a glimpse of the goings-on alongside. This scenario also illustrates why this wasn't the best spot in the world to dispose of a body, unless the perpetrator assumed hurling the suitcase over the railing meant it would land in mud, or water, and be washed away.

Letecia's Movements on January 28th, 2020

"Always mystify, mislead and surprise the enemy if possible." — Stonewall Jackson

A t 08:17 Letecia searches Priceline.com for a good deal on a rental car. Shortly after that she goes to pick one up.

On the morning of January 28, 2020, Letecia rented a 2019 Kia Rio from <u>Avis Rent-A-Car in Colorado Springs</u>. Letecia picked Mr. Stauch up at the Colorado Springs Airport at or about 08:50…shortly after Letecia rented the vehicle. Letecia and Mr Stauch drove back to their residence from the airport in the rented Kia. – Stauch Affidavit, page 8

The timestamp on the <u>invoice from Budget</u> lists a white Kia Rio rented at 08:50 on January 28th. The pick-up location is redacted, but it's likely <u>the Budget branch at the Colorado Springs Airport</u> [the other two franchises are both to the north of Colorado Springs, in the general vicinity of where Gannon's body was initially dumped.] So it's possible the "Avis" reference in the affidavit is an error, especially since the only Avis branch in Colorado Springs is about a block away from the Sheriff's office.

The Stauch Affidavit emphasizes the *timing of the rental* of the Kia as suspicious. Interestingly, the Kia is white. Is this merely a coincidence?

Many rental cars are white, if not most. Or did Letecia purposefully select a particular kind of vehicle, and a particular color?

Perhaps Letecia thought the authorities might <u>confuse the white Kia</u> with her daughter's <u>white Jetta</u>. Conversely, perhaps she wanted a car completely opposite to her <u>black SUV</u> and she wasn't thinking about her daughter's vehicle at all. Without seeing the Kia and Harley's vehicle side-by-side it's hard to say, but given the unusual importance of a whole fleet of different vehicles in this case, and the enduring mystery of the boy's disposal, perhaps these details may prove to be significant.

Even more suspicious than the timing of the rental is the sneaky move of leaving the Tiguan at the airport throughout Tuesday.

According to Page 8 of the Stauch Affidavit:

The Tiguan remained parked in the Colorado Spring's Airport Short Term Parking until approximately 19:00 on January 28…

Curiously, the Tiguan was back on the road, back in service even *while the Kia was still being rented.* In other words, the Kia [or some other vehicle] was used to return to the airport, Letecia then changed cars and headed out of the airport in the Tiguan at about 19:00, about an hour and 44 minutes after sunset that day.[7]

Before we deal with where Letecia went on the night of January 28th, let's examine three important psychological aspects leading up to the disposal:

1. Letecia's reason for hiring the Kia

Letecia was in a race against time after murdering the 11-year-old in his bedroom. She had to get rid of the evidence before a pair of children, one eight [her stepdaughter Laina], the other seventeen [her

---

7 Sunset on Tuesday, January 28th, 2020 was at 17:16 in Colorado Springs.

biological daughter Harley, who also had a car and fulltime job], arrived home.

Laina was easy to manage. Letecia just had to insist her stepdaughter step outside the house almost as soon as she arrived home. Harley wasn't as easy, but if she gave Harley her car[8] and sent her on an errand the moment *she* got home [for cleaning supplies Letecia needed more of anyway], well that was hitting a few birds with one stone, wasn't it?

The psychology behind hiring the Kia worked the same way. As soon as Al arrived, she could get rid of Gannon.

When Al was there, Gannon would be here. When Al was here, Gannon would be there.

Letecia could hide the movements of her vehicle behind the plausible deniability of going to pick up Al from the airport. And if she picked up the vehicle at the airport, the vehicle switcheroo would be known only to those close to her.

So the reason behind hiring the Kia really had to do with Al's arrival. Once he got home and found out Gannon was gone, Al was going to turn the place upside down looking for him, and that likely included her car.

Letecia had had time to do a thorough job of cleaning up the bloodbath in Gannon's bedroom [and bloody mattresses and carpets are amongst the toughest crime scenes to conceal]. But, unluckily for her, because she'd created a bloodbath she'd used all her time cleaning up her homicidal mess. This meant, before Al's arrival the next morning, there was no time left over to get rid of Gannon's bloodied corpse.

---

8 The Stauch Affidavit isn't clear about which vehicle Harley took when she departed on Monday afternoon for the Dollar store. A receipt from the Dollar store dated January 27th, 2020 and timestamped 17:14 was found inside the Tiguan.

2.   Where to put Gannon's Body before Al gets home?

On Monday night when the cops came to sniff around, Gannon was likely in a brown suitcase,[9] inside a cardboard box, inside garbage bags, inside the trunk of the black Volkswagen Tiguan.

We can be fairly certain about this because blood traces[10] belonging to Gannon were found in the garage in the area below the rear hatch of the Tiguan, as well as positive Blue Star reagent reactions for blood on the Tiguan's rear bumper.

Since the cops arrived late,[11] at 22:09, they only searched the house. By then, the whiff of bleach and signs of furious cleaning had no doubt fizzled into the ether. The Tiguan, unusually, was inside the garage when the El Paso Sheriff's officers went through the house. Searching in the dark, and on a bitterly cold night, meant they didn't spend an excess amount of time at the scene. What were they doing? They were looking for a young runaway. A black vehicle in a blackened garage late on an icy cold night, with two vehicles parked outside, wouldn't have been at the top of the officer's search list, would it?

Just as in the JonBenét Ramsey case, the Patrick Frazee case and the Watts case, a preliminary search by the cops yielded nothing. That's because the cops weren't looking for a dead body even though one was, or had been, in the house. In the Watts case, we saw how long it took for anyone to look in the trunk of the Lexus, or, for that matter, inside his Ford Lariat truck.

---

9 The use of the suitcase to hide Gannon's body may have had something to do with the programming involved of Al returning from a trip with suitcases that would have to be loaded into her vehicle.

10 Letitia would later say this blood was a result of Gannon cutting his foot.

11 EPSO arrived three hours after Letecia's 911 call.

If hiding Gannon's body in the Tiguan worked with the kids and cops on Monday night, Letecia knew she had to get rid of it before Al got home. But how? It made sense to leave the vehicle at the airport when she collected Al, so that when they got home, Gannon's body would be safe and out of sight in the Tiguan, at the airport.

According to page 8 of the Stauch Affidavit, Al together with investigators, searched fruitlessly for the Tiguan. At this stage Letecia wouldn't say where the car was, choosing to lie instead. According to the affidavit:

During the time period Letecia had the Kia, she would not provide the location of the Tiguan...She told Mr. Stauch the Tiguan was <u>near French Elementary School</u>.

3. Letecia's explanation to Al – about the rental

On Tuesday morning, Letecia arrived at the Colorado Springs Airport[12] at about 08:30 in the Tiguan. She departed about 20 minutes later in the white Kia with Al and his luggage. Did Al ask about the Kia? Or did Letecia volunteer a prepared explanation? Probably the latter. Letecia justified renting the Kia because she said she was worried about putting mileage[13] onto her Tiguan, which was a leased vehicle.

We don't know what Al made of this half-baked excuse. Possibly Al wasn't all that familiar with Letecia's movements, or methods, and since he was under the impression Letecia was starting a new job, perhaps he assumed there might be some merit to Letecia's financial calculus. Even so, Al's focus that morning was more likely on Gannon than on Letecia's ditzy car rental and mileage calculations. Ironically,

---

12 Letecia dropped Al off at Denver International airport at the beginning of his trip.

13 The mileage lie is ironic given where Gannon's remains ultimately turned up.

the answer to where Gannon was and what had happened to him had *everything* to do with the apparently random rental entering the picture at this point.

Letecia's belief that she could pull the wool over people's eyes reveals a lot about her psychology, and her attitude to reality. The fact that Letecia could murder a child in his own bedroom, especially in the way that she did, and then brazenly hide his murder from the child's family suggests Letecia was used to getting away with petty lies and deceits, and some not so petty. Not all liars are murderers, but all murderers are liars. As this narrative will demonstrate, Letecia, like Chris Watts, was a habitual liar but not a particularly accomplished one. Given the length of time it took to arrest the 36-year-old stepmother, compared to Watts, she appears to have more game than Watts. The question is how much more? A little more or a lot?

We know for sure Letecia spent a lot of time fording through the untested swarms of social media. On social media you can make claims, or statements, or arguments, and no one is really going to press you for evidence, no one is going to really test your posts for bullshit, or hold up a prior version that didn't really make sense. In other words, the standards for a story or a scheme holding water in the make-believe or make-it-up networks of social media [like MLM] are a lot lower than say, a police investigation.

Also, <u>based on Letecia's online searches</u>, one has the impression Al didn't pay much attention to Letecia anyway. This may have given Letecia the idea that she could get away with something big, because she was getting away with a lot of small things, right under Al's nose.

Perhaps Al's inattention was because he was busy, perhaps it was because the marriage was no longer on a sure footing, or perhaps Al didn't pay much attention to Letecia because she was a bullshitter;

always bullshitting him. The Eguardo Fiction[14] suggests Letecia's bullshitting knew few bounds, doesn't it?

Maybe Al knew the mileage thing was a ruse but didn't particularly care. Maybe Letecia was so confident of her ability as a con artist, with her husband and others, that she thought this whopper would fly too. But <u>the distance to the airport from 6627 Mandan Drive</u> is only eight miles. According to the affidavit, Letecia put on a total of 71 miles onto the Tiguan during the period the Kia was leased. What this reveals is that it travelled roughly 30-35 miles to wherever Gannon was disposed of,[15] assuming Letecia left the airport at 19:02 on the 28th, drove straight to a disposal site, and then came straight back. That *is* precisely what she did.

____

14 The Eguardo Fiction was a story Letecia told to the cops on January 29th, of being raped during the incident by a Hispanic male. It appears on pages 11 - 14 of the <u>Stauch Affidavit</u> [points 82 to 101].

15 Gannon was initial dumped in an area close to Palmer Lake, in <u>the deserted northern outskirts of Colorado Springs</u>.

Letecia Goes AWOL on the night of January 28th

"Blinding ignorance does mislead us. O! Wretched mortals, open your eyes!" — *Leonardo da Vinci*

At 19:02 on the night of January 28th, the black Volkswagen Tiguan exits Short Term Parking at Colorado Springs Airport. Over the course of the next 17 hours,[16] it will have clocked exactly 71 miles. So, where did it go?

The distance from the Short Term Parking lot, at the airport, to Palmer Lake is 35.5 miles, or 41 minutes' drive. If Letecia dropped Al in Denver[17] so that he could be at Denver International Airport first thing on the 26th, Letecia would have taken <u>the exact same semi-rural road.</u>

---

16 The blood-spattered, foul-smelling Tiguan [which had served as the boy's coffin for 30 long hours], didn't return home on the 28th after leaving the airport. In fact, the Tiguan never returned to Mandan Drive again. At 22:26 on the 28th Letecia asked Harley to come pick her up in the area of Powers and Carefree, about a mile to the north and west of Colorado Springs Airport. On the 29th, at noon, when Letecia finally arrived for an interview with the cops, her vehicle was impounded.

17 It's assumed that Letecia dropped Al in Denver, since he left his truck at home and didn't fly back to the same airport. However, some uncertainty exists around who chauffeured Al to Denver on Saturday night. According to Letecia, an unnamed relative drove Al to Denver and/or dropped Al at the airport. Letecia told *CrimeOnline* in late February:

So, certainly if she'd driven Al to Denver three days prior, or from the drive to Garden of the Gods[18] which Letecia did <u>on Sunday, when Laina, Gannon and herself went hiking</u>, or from the two trips to Petco [again, in the same area], Letecia would have known the terrain. She would have been familiar with the road, known how empty the countryside was, and had a rough idea how long it took going there and back.

On Tuesday night while she was AWOL, her family were at home, so she couldn't be gone much longer than say, 90 minutes.[19]

Driving through the snow-covered countryside at night, alone in her black car, the aim of the game was simple: *stay invisible.* Even more important – she needed to put the dead boy's body somewhere where it wouldn't come back to haunt her. She had to make sure of that. Trouble was, she didn't have much time, she didn't have an *exact* disposal spot figured out and doing this under the cover of night had another draw-back – she couldn't see what she was doing.

Page 25 of the Stauch Affidavit suggests Letecia got lost, or disori-entated in the dark, during her disposal sortie:

*Letecia disposed of Gannon's remains at night-time, and likely was nervous about the location she chose, and **may not have remembered exactly where she dumped Gannon's remains.**[20]*

"[Al] left Saturday night to fly out of the Denver Airport with a family member who had a red eye fly and he had an early morning flight [the next day]."
The <u>Stauch Affidavit</u> confirms this. Page 3 notes:
[Al] spent the night in Denver, on January 25, 2020…[Al] departed via commercial airline on January 26, 2020 [from Denver International Airport]…
18 Garden of the Gods is 22 miles due south of Palmer Lake, and about the same distance to the Stauch residence on Mandan drive.
19 Letecia left the airport at 19:02 and arrived home just after 23:00 on the night of January 28th. She was AWOL for approximately four hours.
20 Coverage in *CrimeOnline* confirms the possibility that Letecia got lost from Letecia herself:

In her haste, aggravated by paranoid hysteria, Letecia managed to leave behind Gannon's sock as well a stain of Gannon's blood soaked into a piece of particle-board by the roadside.[21] Having concluded the disposal, she hightailed it home, exhilarated but also worried. In the dark, diamonds approached from the front, their lights sweeping stars over shimmering snow, while rubies blinked at her up ahead. Letecia reviewed the events of the day.

At **08:48**, on the way to pick up Al, she'd texted Harley:

Pull your car into the garage.

Perhaps in the bright morning light of Tuesday morning, when Letecia drove to the airport to pick up Al, she'd noticed blood at the rear of the Tiguan, and that meant blood may have dropped onto the garage floor. [It had]. While the Tiguan was at the airport, the garage space was open and perhaps blood traces were plainly visible. If they were, she didn't want Al, or anyone else, to see them.

Letecia explained [that] her whereabouts may seem confusing because she "took the back roads" that morning, "because there had been a wreck." Letecia said at one point, she got lost and had to turn around. Letecia said she took exit 163, off of Highway 105, but couldn't remember the exact time.

21 The recovery of Gannon's body was likely just as hasty as the disposal. The bloody sock was likely left behind when Gannon's remains were quickly bundled back into the Nissan Altima on the afternoon of January 30th. It's unclear where the particle-board was sourced. It may have come from the Stauch garage. In this regard, according to *The Sun*:

Letecia claimed the bloody wood [was] a result of several accidents that happened inside the garage...her family frequently loaded leftover boards [which] Albert used for his woodworking hobby, into their pickup truck. Since the boards weren't secured on the truck, she [suggested] they could have easily flown out of the back as she was driving.

Letecia explained Gannon's blood on the board could have come from Gannon's frequent nosebleeds.

"There was some [of Gannon's blood] in the garage. But there are accidents all the time, nosebleeds. Gannon walked around sometimes with blood on his arm from nosebleeds."

At **16:04** she'd expressed concerns to Al.

LETECIA [via text]: *Something isn't right I think they are hiding something.*

Talk about irony.

AL: *Who? The police?*

LETECIA: *Yes. They asked for tooth brushes.*

Al [Sounding unconvinced]: *Hmm. What do u think they're hiding?*

Now, during the drive home, Letecia's still worried about that damned request for tooth brushes.

They think he's dead. That's why they want his DNA.

Page 26 of the Stauch Affidavit indicates that Letecia arrived at the disposal site at 21:22, less than two miles north of Palmer Lake, at a sharp kink in highway 105. At this stage she'd put 37.6 miles of the 71 total miles she drove onto the Tiguan's odometer. She departed the area just six minutes later, at 21:28, arriving at the junction of Powers and Carefree about 32 minutes later at close to 22:00. At this point the Tiguan, which had completed 63.9 miles of the 71 mile roundtrip, was parked overnight. It's unclear where exactly, but the area adjacent to the junction is a sea of strip malls and parking lots straddling the highway on both sides.

At 22:26, Harley's cell phone departs 6627 Mandan Drive. It's an 18 minute, 13 mile drive each way, heading north along the eastern fringe[22] of Colorado Springs Airport to get to the junction, before returning the same way. Harley likely picked her mother up just before or just after Letecia sent a long text to the cops.[23]

---

22 The drive to the junction along the western envelope of the airport, through the denser urban fabric, is only one mile longer, so it's conceivable Harley could have taken this route as well.

23 Even though Letecia summoned Harley to pick her up, it's unclear whether Letecia returned home in Harley's vehicle that night, or whether Harley drove

20 minutes later, just after 23:00, Letecia likely arrived home from her despicable errand – disposing of the child's body – and made sure to wash herself. The car would need a good washing, and airing too.

The cops had tried to make contact with Letecia earlier in the day. They arranged for her to come into the station at 10:00 the next morning. Letecia had blood on her hands, literally, as well as the smell of Gannon's death in her vehicle.[24] She was struggling to hold it together.

At **22:45** Letecia texted the cops, her communique bristling with unbridled indignation.

LETECIA: *What do you want from me? Because I have nothing. One of your very own leaked to me what your guys were doing. I did nothing and/or am being set up.[25] I'm not really even sure other than that being told that by another blue with El Paso. I was told I couldn't go home to sleep and on top of that men were sent to a home with a minor female and she was forced to stay there not to even leave for food. Every conversation…I can hear inside. What do you want from me?[26]*

Letecia to wherever the Kia Rio rental had been parked. Probably the latter. It's likely Letecia would have arrived home after the disposal in the rental, because to not do so would be doubly suspicious, especially with another vehicle, the Tiguan, missing at a sensitive stage in the unfolding saga.

24 The low ambient temperatures in Colorado in late January, along with the fact that the Tiguan was outside and exposed [overnight at Colorado Springs Airport in <u>Short Term Parking</u>] would have slowed the production of cadavarine, and lessened the intensity of cadaver odor in the vehicle.

25 Does this message sound like the message of a bullshitter?

26 Detective Bethel [the author of the Stauch Affidavit] responded to Letecia's bullshit with a calm, no bullshit reply.

LETECIA: *What do you want from me?*

BETHEL: *Come in to talk to me. I would just like information to find Gannon.*

~

Letecia's Hypochondria

"I'm a complete hypochondriac. If my heart starts beating a little faster than normal, I think I'm having an attack." — Antonio Banderas

At 09:00 Letecia returns the Kia and collects her Tiguan.[27] She knows she can't pitch up at the Sheriff's Office with the Tiguan in the state it's in. So she misses her 10:00 appointment with Detective Bethel.

The cops call her to find out what's going on.

Are you still coming in? Where are you?

Letecia speaks to the cops several times that morning. She's adamant that she doesn't want the cops coming to her home. Even at this early stage, the cops are finding her slippery. Page 11 of the Stauch Affidavit notes:

[She] was difficult at best to track down…

What the authorities wanted from Letecia was the truth. And finding Gannon safe and sound. Letecia wasn't able to give them either. Before she could meet with Detective Bethel, Letecia had some urgent

---

27 It's not clear whether the Tiguan spent a second night at Short Term Parking at Colorado Springs Airport. The Stauch Affidavit lists no second time of arrival, or departure, which suggests the Tiguan was parked somewhere else, nearby.

cleaning up to do, including of the Tiguan. She'd also given herself some written homework. When she arrived at the El Paso Sheriff's Office two hours late at noon on Wednesday, the Tiguan's odometer counter ticked over the final miles, stopping the clock at 71.[28] Bizarrely, Letecia even had prepared notes with her, something few police officers had ever seen before.

<u>Pages 12</u> and <u>13</u> of the Stauch Affidavit deal with Letecia's bullshit story about Eguardo. Although we'll deal with this section of the timeline again in the next chapter, which deals with the lead-up to her first television interview, for now it suffices to highlight two important insights from the interview:

1. *Letecia claimed the first thing she did when she arrived home at 14:30 was she disarmed the home security system and went into the basement, and* **Eguardo was there.**

In fact a neighbor's surveillance footage showed the exact time Letecia and Gannon arrived home: 14:19. The door sensor indicated they entered the residence three minutes later, at 14:22. The same surveillance footage showed Laina returning home with the school bus, at 15:11.

Letecia, both as a stepmom and an assistant teacher, would have been well aware of when Laina usually got back from school. She figured less-than-an-hour was plenty of time to do away with Gannon.

---

28 Independent True Crime Rocket Science calculations, based on all the times and locations provided by the affidavit, <u>mapped a total "fastest route" journey by the Tiguan of 73.1 miles</u>. The 2.1 mile discrepancy can be explained by the Tiguan taking a few short cuts. The fastest route, identified by Google Maps, isn't necessarily the shortest route. Also, <u>the unknown overnight parking location</u> near the junction could have marginally reduced the overall final leg of the trip [to the carwash and Sheriff's Office] on the morning of January 29. A theoretical overnight parking site on the west side of the highway, such as <u>the Texas Roadhouse lot</u>, along with <u>a short cut zigzagging through the urban fabric of Colorado Springs</u>, reduces the overall distance down to <u>72.2 miles</u>.

In her bogus story to Detective Bethel she goes down into the basement and Eguardo is there. Eguardo is basically a fictional representation of the Other Side of Letecia. Instead of telling the detective what happened, Letecia conjures an interloper, and *recasts herself as a victim* instead of Gannon.

Whatever Letecia was doing, she wasn't done with the devil's work when her eight-year-old stepdaughter arrived home. When the cops interviewed Laina to verify Letecia's story, Laina told them Letecia told her *Gannon was asleep in her bed.* She couldn't see him. Laina was told to go outside and play.[29] A neighbor's surveillance footage confirms that Laina left the house on her bicycle, and further, that no one else – not Eguardo, no one – entered it.

2. *Letecia claimed she was **in one place**, the basement, for approximately an hour…*

In the Eguardo Fiction Letecia anchors herself in the timeline to the basement. She's stuck there for a long time against her will because she's being raped. The Eguardo Fiction is a psychological nod to what actually happened to Gannon. What he experienced, the penetration of sharp objects into his body, causing him to bleed, is a kind of psychological admission of what Letecia imagines as *the rape and destruction of a human body.*

The reference to "blacked out" after hitting her head is likely a reference to Gannon passing away, either because of bleeding out or from a gunshot wound to the head.

If a stabbing weapon *and* gun was used, this may be because it was assumed Gannon would quickly and easily die after being stabbed, stabbing being preferable to the loud noise of a gunshot, which might

---

29 Letecia claimed she went to the garage and helped Laina onto her bike and out into the driveway.

alert neighbors or pedestrians outside. Instead, his murder was clumsy, ineffective and tortuous, much like the disposal of his remains. A stabbing also corresponds to a bloodbath, although a head or neck wound from a bullet might leave behind similar volumes of blood. It's not clear at the time of writing whether Gannon was shot or not,[30] but given Letecia was the wife of <u>a military man</u>, and <u>had some shooting practise</u>, and that she mentions a gun in her fiction, it's conceivable that a gun was the murder weapon.

In the end though it was relatively easy to disprove Letecia's bullshit story. Point 98 on page 13 of the Stauch Affidavit refers to the ADT security logs:

The logs…indicate significant activity in the basement of the residence where evidence suggests Gannon was murdered…On January 27, 2020, the average number of basement motion events was 10.3. The average for the preceding four days was 3.5.

The affidavit suggests this increase in activity was from Letecia running upstairs and downstairs repeatedly to clean the scene, and get of bloodied paper towels, stained bedding, blood-spattered socks and other evidence.

If Letecia crying rape, and blaming a fictional rapist when she's interviewed by the cops isn't a clear sign of hypochondria, what happened next certainly is. As the interview with the cops wrapped up, and as it became clear the cops were onto her – seizing her phone, impounding her car, detaining her and applying for a warrant to get a DNA sample from her – Letecia suddenly develops chest pain and shortness of breath.

According to the Stauch Affidavit:

---

30 At the time of writing autopsy results were unavailable.

Letecia began stuffing tissues in her pants…Investigators immediately requested medical assistance, and paramedics from the Colorado Springs Fire Department arrived.…Paramedics questioned her…Letecia was [then] transported to the hospital via ambulance [but] accompanied by [ESPO] Detectives…to the hospital…Letecia was unresponsive to medical personnel, and seemed to have a miraculous recovery when they arrived at the hospital.

Think about what's happening. Unlike Chris Watts who was stuck in a cubicle for countless hours, and at the mercy of his interrogators, Letecia has found a way out – not only out of the cubicle, but out of the police station, and ultimately, out of police custody. Unluckily for her the cops stick to her like glue, at least in the beginning they do. They even audio record the ambulance ride.

At the hospital Letecia continues to be evasive. Letecia refuses treatment from a Sexual Assault Nurse Examiner who's on hand to examine the alleged "rape." Then she makes a phone call from the hospital waiting room, surreptitiously signs herself out and leaves. Sneakily, she slips out of the hospital without telling the cops.

Like clockwork she's picked up outside by an "unknown person" and is soon reunited her with her daughter a few miles from the hospital. By the time the warrant arrives at the hospital, Letecia's gone.

The Lead-Up to the Sermon on the Verge

"But I say unto you, That whosoever is angry with his brother without a cause shall be in danger of the judgment." — Sermon on the Mount, Matthew 5:22, King James Bible

On Thursday, January 30th, Landen Hiott [Gannon's biological mother] and Al Stauch both give statements and plead for the safe return of their little boy. <u>Landen's distress is sketched all over her face</u>. Al on the other hand seems dazed and subdued.

<u>LANDEN</u>: *I'm Landen Hiott, Gannon's mom. My kid has a life and it's important to me. It's important to everybody that's standing in this room. Gannon, Bubba, Little Man, Mommy's Hero, wherever you're at, mommy and daddy's here. And we're begging and pleading for you to come home….I can't wait until you are found, because I have hope you are gonna be found. You are my hero. You are the reason why I have life. He's so special to me. I don't think many people could understand, my child was a one pound, six ounce baby. He had a 10% chance of survival. None of that happened. He's gifted and talented. Do anything for anybody. So I'm begging, I'm pleading, if anybody has any type of lead, put yourself in my situation. Ask yourself, what would you do…Please have*

hope with me. I'm beggin'. [Sniffs]. Bring my baby home. Bubba Momma loves you, Momma loves you so much.

Landen mentions that his sister loves him, and the room is full of love, so please come home. Landen's assuming Gannon's status as a runaway is true. That's what Letecia told the cops, that he'd left home and not come back. He'd run away. Ironically, running away was what she was about to do.

AL [Pinching his nose with his fingers]: *I want to reiterate what Landen said. Wow, what an incredible community we have…I came out my front door, I think it was Tuesday, and there was 300 people out there searching my neighborhood. [Sounds tearful] Blew-blew me away. [Pinches his nose, weeps]. So thank you everyone, [voice breaks] thank you. And…Gannon daddy loves you so much. Please come home. [Al and Landen embrace beside the press podium].*

In all, Landen's heartfelt appeal to the community lasts about two minutes twenty seconds, and Al's about one minute. So it's in the context of a unified Landen and Al that the stepmother decides to hold her own press conference on the side of the road. Her choice of venue, the side of the road with rising subdivisions and the snow-spattered Rockies visible over her shoulders, is ironic, isn't it? It's dislocated, rootless, and in a sense, without an anchor or a context. Letecia, wearing dark glasses, has her back to the camera. This is another contrast from Gannon's parents' genuine appeal the day prior.

Letecia's Sermon on the Verge takes place four days after her 11-year-old stepson went missing while in her care, and immediately after Landen and Al's public appeal. It lasts a full ten minutes, but it's not so much what she says or does that stands out. It's the amount of extraneous information Letecia provides and what she *doesn't* say, or do, that irks. Let's listen in.

LETECIA: *I am Tecia Stauch, which is Gannon's stepmother.*

Tecia?[31] Why doesn't Letecia identify herself by her full name?[32] And why the strange "which is" language? Why not say it like it is [or how it's supposed to be]:

I'm Gannon's stepmom.

Own it.

Stepmother is also not the sort of term that Letecia owns in the same way Landen own's her motherhood when she addresses the crowd.

Something else to notice is a lack of emotion in Letecia's opening words. We can't see her face, but we can hear her voice, and the tone of it in her very first words sounds as if she's gearing up to make an excuse.

<u>REPORTER</u>: *You've been a part of the investigation [from the start]; you were the last person to see him, is that right?*

LETECIA: *Correct.*

REPORTER: *What did you see when you last saw him?*

LETECIA: *Well, I'm not allowed to talk about anything with the case.*

So Letecia is being evasive from the first question after establishing her name, sort of. Now, compare this to Chris Watts during his Sermon on the Porch. He was asked about the last time he saw Shan'ann and the kids, and he was quite clear about it.

In a missing persons case, everyone – cops, the community, family – want to know as much as they possibly can about the last moments

---

31 We'll spend more time dealing with how Letecia identifies herself and spells her name through the course of this narrative.

32 Letecia Stauch turning her back to the camera is done to protect her identity. The shortened version of her name instead of clearly identifying herself, is intended to do the same thing – protect her identity. Why does the stepmom want to protect her identity when the real emergency is that her stepson is missing?

someone was seen. Letecia's response, right here, reveals that this is a lot more serious than the actual status of the case. It reflects she has inside knowledge of the case. The whole scenario of appearing in front of the cameras to make a statement, but then to not really do that, and to turn her back on the camera is evasive and misleading. So why is Letecia doing it? Well, isn't it because that's what this is all about – trying to mislead?

The difference between Letecia and Chris Watts is, Watts didn't volunteer to do his Sermon on the Porch. He didn't call up or invite a phalanx of reporters to interrogate him. What's astonishing is Letecia seems to have thought about this, and has gone out of her way to speak to one reporter.

Page 11 of the Stauch Affidavit provides some context for this moment of engagement with the media.

On January 29, 2020 [two days prior to her Sermon on the Verge] Letecia voluntarily came to the El Paso Sheriff's Office [EPSO] for an interview with investigators, but only after she was evasive and avoided speaking with investigators one-on-one. Her interview was audio and video recorded [but], in general, her statements are reasonably categorized as untruthful, incomplete, and misleading.

As mentioned earlier, Letecia was meant to arrive at the Sherriff's office at 10:00 on the 29th, but elected to arrive at noon instead.

The Stauch Affidavit further states that although Letecia spoke to investigators frequently over the phone:

She did not want investigators coming to her home, [33] *and was difficult at best to track down...Letecia brought several pieces of notebook*

---

33 Letecia likely had a good reason for wanting to keep the cops out of her home. There were blood trails to clean up, and odors associated with bleach and vinegar that needed to dissipate and disappear. She also needed to get the VW Tiguan washed.

paper [to the interview] and referred to these notes, and asked investigators if she could just read her notes.

Once again, this appears to be someone who may have studied the Watts case, after all it played out and made headline news in the same state. Surely Letecia didn't want to make the same mistake walking into an interrogation cubicle like Watts did, and never walking out again. She wanted to keep her story straight, but the efforts to do so were exposing her paranoia and making the cops suspicious, and rightly so.

Now we can see why Watts playing it cool, and coy, was actually a better strategy at making it seem like nothing serious had happened, and that he wasn't involved. The opposite, second-guessing the cops and being overly-cautious, suited the circumstances even less.

The Stauch Affidavit points out:

It is extremely rare of an individual to bring notes to an interview.

Think about Gannon's parents at the press conference. They're shooting from the hip, telling it like it is. There's no need for prepared statements. But if Letecia had studied the Watts case, she would have known the way agents work is they write down a timeline and get a complete statement from persons of interest. Well, Letecia was beating them to the punch, wasn't she? It may have made sense to her, but in a genuine scenario where Gannon was missing, who would make notes unless there was a story that needed to be manufactured, and kept straight.[34]

Besides note taking and spring cleaning in January, when Letecia showed up to her interview in her Volkswagen Tiguan, they discovered the vehicle was still wet.

The Stauch Affidavit emphasizes in this regard:

---

34 According to page 26 the Stauch Affidavit, by February 14, Letecia ultimately concocted four different story versions to explain what happened to Gannon.

[It appeared] to have been recently cleaned. I submit that Letecia had to clean the vehicle [because of] visible blood on the rear end...Video captured a portion of a black SUV....at 11:30...on January 29 at the car wash[35] <u>located at E Platte/Bonfoy Avenue</u>.

On the 29th, Letecia told the cops she'd been held at gunpoint and raped by a Hispanic named Eguardo. Before the rape, Eguardo allowed Letecia to go upstairs to greet Laina, her stepdaughter. Then, between 15:30 and 16:30[36] Eguardo raped her. Letecia claimed she banged her head and blacked out. But the cops found no evidence of injury to Letecia's head.

Of importance is how Letecia describes the life and death tussle between Eguardo and Gannon. This is from page 12 of the Stauch Affidavit:

*Gannon jumped on Eguardo's back but Eguardo was able to **throw Gannon...across the room.**[37] [Then] Eguardo held a gun to Gannon and demanded a suitcase. Letecia provided him with **a brown suitcase** and a cardbox box. Then Letecia blacked out again [and Eguardo left, doubtless with Gannon]. Once she regained consciousness, Letecia said she cleaned the area where the attack happened, and straightened signs of disturbances in Gannon's room.*

---

35 Letecia likely used <u>Power Wash</u>, a car wash situated right beside the main thoroughfare of E Platte, and conveniently on <u>the way from home to the Sheriff's office</u>.

36 Letecia Stauch's phone records showed she couldn't have been raped if she was texting Al and Harley about headphones at 15:41, 15:42, 15:43, 15:44, 15:45, 16:11, 16:19 and 16:20.

37 In this fictional version it's not clear which room in the house this assault occurred. In reality, we know it was Gannon's bedroom. This is both admitted and muddied via Letecia's story.

One additional point that emerges through the Eguardo Fiction is Letecia admitting that Gannon knocked over a candle on Sunday, causing the carpet to burn. In Letecia's version of events, she met Eguardo who was doing construction work in the neighborhood, asked him to come over and help her to repair the carpet. So we see Letecia acknowledging that **the carpet played a key role as a catalyst for the events** that followed. This is a psychological admission from the stepmother that matches the fabric of the *actual* dynamics.

~

The Sermon on the Verge

"Hope is the great deceiver. Hope is the piper who leads us sleepy to our slaughter." — Brent Weeks, The Broken Eye

The Eguardo Fiction confirmed the worst fears for law enforcement. Letecia's apparently first-hand knowledge of Gannon being flung across the room, hitting a wall, as well as the use of a gun and a brown suitcase all suggested an unhappy ending for Gannon.

The admission within the Eguardo Fiction of an elaborate cleaning exercise prior to calling 911 at 18:55[38] also provided *behavioral* precedent. It showed the tendency of someone actively but furtively covering their tracks before the display of doing the right thing at the appropriate time. And that's what the Sermon on the Verge was all about: a display of manufactured appropriateness.

<u>REPORTER</u>: *You've been a part of the investigation [from the start]; you were the last person to see him, is that right?*

LETECIA: *Correct.*

Yes, but I'm not here to talk about how I am part of the investigation, or Gannon, or the last thing I saw.

---

38 At 16:52, two full hours before calling 911, Letecia instructed her daughter Harley to pick up carpet cleaner, baking soda and trash bags.

REPORTER: *What did you see when you last saw him?*

LETECIA: *Well, I'm not allowed to talk about anything with the case.*

The reporter pushes Letecia to talk about her final, first-hand moments with Gannon. This time she provides an excuse for why she can't. It's really a matter of won't; it's evasion.

LETECIA: *I would, more so, be willing to talk about the community needs to have faith, and continue to work together.*

Letecia's telling the reporter what she's willing to talk about which is indicative of what she's not willing to talk about. She's also admonishing the public to have faith. Faith in what? In her? While she has her back to the camera? Hey guys, trust me, believe me, have faith in me, but don't ask me to ask you that facing the camera.

LETECIA:*…and not make these false accusations.*

Oh, like about Eguardo?

LETECIA:*…like things that have been said, that I've disappeared.*

Well, let's face it, Letecia did disappear on and off, didn't she? She disappeared with Eguardo into the basement for a critical hour, according to her own story. When she was supposed to meet with Detective Bethel she was somewhere else. When the cops wanted to interview her she disappeared from the hospital. On the night of the 28th, she disappeared. Her Tiguan too, disappeared and reappeared as well.

The astonishing thing about this statement is how Letecia is caught up in her own feedback loop. Shouldn't this be about Gannon's disappearance? Instead she's trying to put out fires about her disappearing, and instead of prioritizing the search for Gannon, what's foremost on Letecia's mind are the accusations levelled against her.

LETECIA: *[The community says] I haven't been there to help [voice adopts a lilt here]. But there's lots of reasons behind that.*

Page 23 of the Stauch Affidavit confirms that Letecia hadn't been very helpful, specifically in the search for Gannon:

During the first 24-48 hours surrounding the disappearance of a child, it's reasonable that an innocent person would [contribute] to search efforts, fully participating in the effort to recover the child. In the 24-48 hours surrounding Gannon's disappearance, Letecia rented a vehicle, turned her cell phone off for four hours on the evening of January 28th, washed her Tiguan…evaded law enforcement…and did not participate in the search for Gannon.

So yes, there were many reasons why Letecia hadn't been around to help. Cleaning, covering up, conjuring cars and disappearing tricks take time and effort.

REPORTER: *Uh, reasons like death threats, right?*

LETECIA: *Right. Death threats are one. My family's getting lots of death threats, we counted 20-some, death threats already. Um, too, my husband's ex-wife is living in our home. And of course [bounces slightly to emphasize her indignation] I'm not coming home to do these things, and help with the family when I was kinda like told, I couldn't. Um, and then many other things that happened with the El Paso County Police Department. You know, in doing the investigation, I was told I wasn't complying. Can I elaborate on that?*

REPORTER: *Please do.*

LETECIA: *Yes, so [sighs], I asked for an attorney during the interview, uh, and I was denied that by them. I was held, because they were blocking the door. And I was told I couldn't leave, and if woulda touched them, they woulda said, you know, I still wasn't complying, or said I was, you know, trying to run away or something. But during the interview I asked several times, could I stop the interview, could I get an attorney.*

This seems to be Letecia's bugbear – the police interview. She's here to set the record straight about that. She's the victim. Although it's possible Letecia asked for an attorney and was rebuffed by the cops, since there's no reference to a request for an attorney [a legal protocol law enforcement are sensitive to] in the affidavit, and since Letecia prepared notes implicating a third party for her January 29 interview, it makes no sense that she'd ask for an attorney if her story was that she was the victim of a crime.

One suspects any interview with Letecia was recorded, just as Chris Watts' interrogation was. If the ambulance ride was recorded, surely the police interviews – all of them – were as well. If that's the case it shouldn't be hard to disprove Letecia's claim of being denied a lawyer as a lie. If it is, it's one in a whirling hurricane of noisy, distracting untruths.

If that's what this is, what's Letecia hoping to achieve by lying on camera about an attorney? It's trying to gain or win some sort of public leverage over the cops. In short: she's trying to politicize[39] her situation in order to win over popular support.

LETECIA: *Could I stop the interview, could I get something to drink.*[40] *Could I get an attorney? I was denied. I was told I couldn't get nothing to drink. I was told I couldn't go to the bathroom. I mean it was continuously…that <u>my constitutional rights were violated</u>.*

---

39 <u>Politicizing something</u> means attempting to gain leverage or bias over something. It involves redirecting an opinion, or influencing a view of something along a particular narrow, partisan and necessarily distorted field of focus. In essence, it's an attempt to conjure power over a particular set of circumstances by convincing a group of a particular reality, often in opposition to the objective facts.

40 Point 81 on page 11 of the Stauch Affidavit states:
Investigators provided food and water to Letecia during the interview.

We're 90 seconds into the 10-minute interview and thus far it's all about Letecia. She's taken a while to get to the point: so this is about her constitutional rights. This is about her interests being violated. In a sense this is absolutely correct. Letecia committed this crime, it appears, because she felt her rights [as a person, a wife, a mother] weren't being honoured.

In the *"I'm Bleeding"* chapter we'll revisit the family dynamics, to test whether there's any merit to this theory of Letecia being unhappy about her role in the family situation.

REPORTER: *And that's why you said, they said, you weren't cooperating with the investigation.*

LETECIA: *That's why they said I wasn't cooperating at that time. Correct.*

REPORTER [Sounding unconvinced]: *Then why did you ask for an attorney at the time?*

LETECIA: *Well, I asked for an attorney at the time [flaps out both hands], because there was one individual, or two, really good detectives, so I'm not, you know, gonna talk bad about the detectives. But the tactics they started to get when I would answer questions, they tried tah – you know, they're detectives, they try to twist – their one main goal is to find Gannon.*

Yes, isn't it?

LETECIA [Speaking quickly]: *But during that time, some of those things made me feel uncomfortable. The way they were saying things. So I immediately stopped, and felt like an attorney would help with some of the vocabulary, and things like that, that I needed help with. To understand some of the things that were asking.*

Ohhhh. So she needs help with big words, not because there are any culpability issues, not because she wants a drink of water, or to go to the bathroom. Not because she's in any legal trouble what with

Gannon disappeared while in her custody – it's the semantics she needs to be rescued from.

REPORTER: *I'm gonna shift gears to…what has become a huge online presence of people [bobs head] obviously trying to do the right thing.*

LETECIA: *Right. Mmhm.*

REPORTER: *Help find Gannon. But at the same time, sometimes it just feels like we're no longer [inaudible]. Have you seen any of those comments yourself?*

LETECIA: *We have.*

Not: I have.

We know Letecia's an obsessive smartphone and social media user. It's arguably her continued presence online that caused this case to explode online as much as it has. At this point Letecia was still trying to remote control or remote influence this case. To politicize the situation one way [her way] or the other. Except social media is a funny animal. It's a tough monster to tame. And the more that's out there, the more it can kick you off its back, swallow you whole and spit you out.

LETECIA: *See, that's one of the main things…we haven't been in the public eye…because I didn't want to expose my family to it.*

Who is Letecia's family at this point? It's not Al. It's not Laina. Is it her and Harley?

LETECIA: *You know there were comments about Gannon being pushed off the hike, and there were comments about this, and that's just not true. I took care of Gannon, for the last two years, in our home.*

This part's true: **I took care of Gannon…in our home.**

LETECIA: *Cos his mother didn't wanna do it.*

Big gripe here. Big swipe here. And what about Al?

LETECIA: *And I would never, ever, ever hurt this child.*

Letecia has to reinforce her denial, because alone it's not enough.

It's not: *I didn't hurt my son.* It's not: *I didn't hurt Gannon.*

Letecia acknowledges at this point that there are some questions, but pushes it onto the investigators. That's for them to find out. There's a very opportunistic thing going on here, isn't there? Letecia herself should be interested in the search for Gannon. Instead, the last witness who saw him alive is saying let the cops look for him. Why should I?

LETECIA: *I've cooperated with them. Even to the point that we were held with a gun. My daughter, a 17-year-old who serves our country, and the United States Air Force, who has never committed a crime, or done anything wrong in her life, was put in handcuffs over the keys that was in her purse. So they could take her car.*

REPORTER: *They weren't in her car.*

LETECIA: *They weren't even in her car, I mean in her purse. They were in my pocket.*

A nasty little slip of the tongue here. Things obviously were in cars that shouldn't have been in cars. Things that could get you charged with murder.

REPORTER: *You originally didn't know it was a...law enforcement...officer?*

<u>LETECIA</u>: *I didn't know he was a law enforcement officer, because when he came out I guess he was putting his jacket on. It wasn't necessarily his fault; he was adjusting and happened to catch me. But I saw the gun, and I panicked [throw out both arms, hands flayed like wings], originally. And kinda...thought, oh gosh...who is this guy? And then, once I realized it was a Sheriff's office...I was totally okay, but they still had a gun, and they told me they were gonna shoot me. But I was very concerned about my daughter; asking why she was being detained, in handcuffs, and things like that. When: that shouldn't even happen for a child. That shouldn't even*

happen for someone who standing inside of a store, shopping. Cos we didn't have any clothes, cos all of our clothes were here...

Letecia seems genuinely concerned about her daughter, and perhaps with some justification. The Stauch Affidavit acknowledges that Harley didn't seem to be a knowing accessory, even though Harley was often part of her mother's plans, and obviously went to buy the cleaning supplies. It's difficult to imagine, listening to Letecia, that all of this is happening because Gannon is missing. Gannon's name has hardly been mentioned.

LETECIA: *She was put in handcuffs in the store...and brought out with guns. That's just not okay. They coulda approached me and said, 'Hi, I'm with El Paso county, can I please get this,' instead of the way that it happened.*

At almost halfway through the Sermon on the Verge, the reporter steps out of the shot for a moment, ostensibly to make sure the recording is okay – it is – and then shifts gear again. He wants Letecia to address rumors online that Letecia's not involved enough in the search for Gannon. Big reaction now from Letecia. What people are saying about her on social media seems to be a lot worse for her than what the cops are saying, or doing.

<u>LETECIA</u>: *Ooh! Oh yes, wow. The rumors have gotten so bad. Uh...I pretty much have been told, at least ten different ways, that these people have these conspiracy theories. I guess they watch a lot of law shows; and maybe they have all these theories...how...[takes a breath] Gannon-is-dead [spoken rapidly and under her breath]. And that's what they're saying. [Waves her hand, raises her voice]. So I'm like: Why are you saying Gannon is dead? He is not dead. We are gonna find Gannon.*[41]

---

41 The above analysis covers about 50% of the <u>Sermon on the Verge</u>. The next narrative *The Trial of Letecia Stauch* analyzes the remaining 50%.

The Search for Gannon

"Police thought he'd run away, but now they believe something else has happened, and he could be in danger." — <u>CBS Denver</u>, *31 January, 2020*

On the same day Gannon's status changed from missing to endangered [Friday, January 31st, the day of the Sermon on the Verge], <u>the FBI joined the search for Gannon</u>. At this stage the El Paso Sheriff's Department had received 72 tips, and were appealing to the public for more information. The same day Bloodhounds searched an area east of Colorado Springs, to no avail.

They're gonna find Gannon.

It's just a matter of time.

Locals and law enforcement rallied at the end of January, and early February, pooling resources in a combined search for the missing 11-year-old. Hundreds volunteered. Drones, dogs, folks on horseback – all joined in the search for the boy. Days turned into weeks. As the weeks went on it seemed less and less certain to law enforcement, and to the searchers, that Gannon would be found. They were also becoming more and more convinced that foul play was involved.

For Letecia, it was different. As the days went on, and the searches intensified, it seemed more and more certain Gannon *would* inevitably be found.

We are gonna find Gannon.

Not long – hours – after her Sermon on camera, Letecia reflected.

They're gonna find Gannon. Unless I do somethin', they're gonna find Gannon.

From the affidavit it appears Letecia realized early on that Gannon's dead body would be found unless she found it, and moved it first. But finding and recovering and then hiding what she'd meant to hide permanently proved more challenging than the 36-year-old had likely bargained for.

Letecia obsessively studied the news about her. She searched for news about searches. Where were they searching? Searches were going on all over the place. Every day the search was somewhere else. More and more folks in the community were volunteering. Then the searches started zeroing in on <u>a site in southern Douglas County</u>.

They know something.

They found something.

All of this activity was too close for comfort. To Letecia's credit, she got spooked by the searches very early on, which was why she able to pull the wool over the eyes of law enforcement, and the community searching, for as long as she did. Most of the searches in February were for someone – something – that was *no longer there*. The question arises: how early was Gannon's corpse removed? It now appears as if the body lay outside, under a pile of snow[42] not far from the roadside, for no more than *three days*.

Now, let's go back to January 31st…

---

42 The fact that the body was under snow meant cadaver traces, including cadaver odor, would be minimal. Burying the body under snow was akin to storing the body in a freezer.

Since her Tiguan was still impounded, and unbeknown to her, its computer chip undergoing analysis, the day after her brush with the law, Letecia rented another vehicle: a <u>2020 Nissan Altima</u>, on January 30th.[43] At this stage Gannon's body had been outside for almost two full days.

On the 31st, when Letecia gave her 10-minute-long Sermon on the Verge, it's likely Harley and at least one other person were sitting in the silver Altima. At an unknown interval after the interview, Letecia felt an irresistible urge to check on, and perhaps recover Gannon's body.

According to page 24 of the Stauch Affidavit:

Investigators believe Letecia utilized the rented Nissan Altima to return to the area in which she disposed of Gannon's body.

The Altima arrived at GPS coordinates 39.21486 -104.929172 in the area north of Palmer Lake [about 47 miles north-north-west of the Stauch home] at exactly 16:16. It then backtracked south 7 miles to a wooded section of road, arriving at 39.140 – 104.913 at 16:41. The Altima then headed north to 39.190 -104.894 arriving at 16:58. The Altima lingered in the area, possibly leaving the main road and the ability of mapping technology to track, until at least 17:13. After an hour in which the body was either moved or recovered, the Altima returned to an undisclosed location in Colorado Springs.

It's assumed that close to this date Gannon's remains were transported out of Colorado state entirely. Because of this, systematic, strategic searches backed up by strong, digital intel, would come up almost empty handed over the next few weeks.

---

43 Letecia rented the Nissan Altima for three days, between January 30th and February 1st.

Letecia's Next Statement: "I feel the need to fill in some gaps"

Letecia has received significant criticism online, with many accusing her of being involved in Gannon's disappearance. – <u>KDVR</u>, February 12th, 2020

In the first days of February, one person is keeping track of the search for Gannon far more than anyone else. She's scouring social media constantly for news, but not because she wants Gannon found. She's terrified something, some smidgeon she's forgotten about, might be found and traced back to her. Because of what she's done she has reason to worry. This person watching everything that's happening like a hawk online, is Letecia herself.

Such insatiable, obsessive compulsive scrutiny can be an Achilles heel. The affidavit refers to Letecia's heavy use of social media and online tools, citing her unusual *curiosity*.[44] Could this be used against her?

On February 4th, a Tuesday, four days after Friday's Sermon on the Verge, the <u>neighbor's surveillance video was leaked to the media</u>. Headlines and <u>stills taken from the surveillance</u>, like this one from <u>KDVR</u> –

---

44 Point 140 on page 21 refers to Letecia's motive, and in this respect highlights how her online searches "memorialize" and "shed light on" her "inquisitive" nature.

Surveillance footage could provide clues in search for missing El Paso County boy – had to send chills down Letecia's spine, and perhaps that was the point.

The next day, Wednesday, February 5th, Gannon's family [Al, Landen and Laina] made a tearful plea.[45] Interestingly, the plea was posted onto social media – on El Paso County's official YouTube channel – rather than through traditional broadcast media.

Gannon's mother pointedly observed:

"A kid doesn't just disappear and no one sees him."[46]

A statement like this poured cold water on Letecia's claim that Gannon had gone to a friend, and on his original status [based on Letecia's initial statement] that he was a runaway. The leaked video and the plea seemed designed to put pressure on Letecia specifically, and perhaps someone close to her, just as the Sermon on the Porch was engineered for the same reason in the Chris Watts case. The Thayers, who took Watts in on Tuesday night, mere hours after the Sermon on the Porch aired on national television, bore the brunt of a social media shitstorm. It was so bad they sat down for a half-hour interview that same week to apologize for their mistake, including for placing their own daughter [who slept across the hall from Watts that night] potentially in harm's way.

If we're going to compare the social media in these cases, why not compare the criminal aspects more directly as well?[47]

---

45 An analysis of the Stauch Family Video is available on the TCRS Patreon channel.

46 "A kid doesn't just disappear and no one sees him." Consider this statement in the context of the Madeleine McCann case, and more recently, the Nora Quoirin case.

47 The intertextual aspects between the Watts case and the Stauch case, as well as another high-profile case in Colorado, are covered in more depth in the penultimate chapter.

In the Chris Watts case, Watts confessed to the location of the bodies of his children three days after committing triple murder. How long would searches have gone on had he not confessed? The Stauch case suggests it could have gone on a lot longer. Bear in mind in the Stauch case, the cops *also* had GPS data and yet the searches for Gannon in Colorado came up empty for weeks on end.

If the leaked video and the plea seemed designed to put pressure on Letecia, that pressure clearly worked. Eight days after the video leaked, and seven days after the family's plea, Letecia felt *compelled* to respond. On February 12th, two weeks and a day after Gannon's disappearance, Letecia broke her self-imposed silence, choosing the medium she was most comfortable with to do so.

KDVR quotes Letecia's Facebook post confirming the impact of online speculation on the police's prime suspect in Gannon's disappearance.

Social Media has been devastating *from the harsh comments, speculations, threats, cyber bullying, etc.*

In the same Facebook post Letecia indulged her audience in a few important disclosures – important to her – regarding some of her final moments with Gannon. What was foremost on Gannon's stepmother's mind? Blood. Specifically blood evidence. We know from the affidavit she'd been asked to explain traces of Gannon's blood found all over the house.

So naturally the "gaps" she wanted to fill had to with Gannon's blood.

KDVR quotes Letecia's Facebook post as follows:

*"Please **take a step back** for a moment and **let me explain** to you a few details that were not released."*

Hold on, what happened to:

REPORTER: *What did you see when you last saw him?*

LETECIA: *Well, I'm not allowed to talk about anything with the case.*

Apparently Letecia's giving herself permission to talk about the case now, and in some very specific detail too.

*Please **take a step back** for a moment*

*and **let me explain***

It's not rocket science, the psychology at work here. Letecia wants the curious, inquiring and increasingly suspicious minds to "step back" so she can "explain" – <u>gaslight</u> – the community, the cops, basically everyone. She has inside information, which does make her a valid source on what really happened to Gannon. The question is, *how credible is she as a person*, as a source, and what does she do with this unique insight? Also, think about these words in the context of the poor little boy stuck in the custody of his stepmother, having committed the unforgivable sin of burning the carpet:

*Please **take a step back** for a moment*

*and **let me explain***

By way of explanation, Letecia highlights the neighbor's surveillance video. This, above all, has fuelled suspicion against her. Ironically, the same situation played out in the Watts case, where a grainy, unclear video was used to justify several theories, almost all of which weren't accurate. In Letecia's case **the video also misrepresents what really happened**, even though the basic, underlying aspects are accurate:

1. that she was with Gannon in the truck at some point,

2. returned home at some point and

3. that no one else [not Eguardo, not <u>Quincy Brown</u>] entered the residence.

Letecia's Facebook post continues:

*"For example, just like the video [the neighbor's surveillance footage] that was leaked, there are **additional details that were hidden** due to 1) the department doing its job 2) the effects of social media and how some individuals would criticize or **hinder the investigation. I chose to listen, I didn't leak videos or information**. But at this time it's getting later in the process and we just want Gannon home. I feel the need to fill in some gaps."*

Hold on, once again, what happened to:

REPORTER: *What did you see when you last saw him?*

LETECIA: *Well, I'm not allowed to talk about anything with the case.*

In the broader psychology of the case, where a child has been secretly murdered, the blood cleaned, the body hidden, think about the mirror image behind Letecia's words:

*there are **additional details that were hidden***

*how some individuals would criticize or **hinder the investigation***

***I chose to listen, I didn't leak videos or information**[48]*

What this is is an individual occupying her own reality, and cherry picking words and realities to support, to defend her own. Letecia's giving herself permission to talk about the case now, and in some very specific detail too:

---

48 The signature aspect of the Stauch case is Letecia's strategic leaking of videos and information. Letecia's use of social media to attempt to influence public opinion, and more pertinently, public opinion of her, is one reason for the unprecedented traction of the Stauch case. We saw in Chris Watts case how public sentiment turned on social media commentary, with Shan'ann Watts' social media alternately used to either condemn or lionize her. Since Gannon's disappearance, and until her arrest, Letecia actively made use of social media as a tool to cast herself as an innocent victim. If this isn't an intertextual artefact related to the unusually social-media-heavy Watts case, then it's peculiarly coincidental to it.

"Saturday Night, G was helping me unload in the garage and cut his foot because there are a lot of tools because Albert does woodworking."

G?

Gannon has now been reduced to a letter. This is a classic case of distancing in the sense that even acknowledging the missing boy is reduced, minimized, to a letter.

was helping me

Letecia sketches Gannon in his final moments on January 25th helping her. Clearly, Letecia didn't want to get rid of her stepson because of his helpful nature. Obviously the candle burning incident wasn't her idea of Gannon being helpful either. She uses the word helpful in order to misconstrue the dynamics. She sees him as helpful, he's helping her – thus why would she have a motive, and why would it be her fault if he chose to run away?

unload in the garage

This is vital evidence. The cops by now have told Letecia what they know, what they've found. Letecia is scrambling to explain it. She conjures a benign reality here that matches what the police know, and suspect. Something *was* being unloaded [or rather, loaded] in the garage. And yes, during this loading, Gannon's blood *was* shed.

How?

cut his foot

Gannon cutting his foot is the most harmless injury Letecia can think of. If you're going to get hurt in the most harmless way, what's more harmless than stubbing your toe? But it's devastating to Letecia in her situation – suspected of murder, and hiding the body – that there's evidence of Gannon's blood at all. It's troubling that there's blood in his bedroom, it's devastating that there's blood in the garage, and it's almost incontrovertible when these blood traces then continue to Letecia's vehicle – the same vehicle that went AWOL on the 28th.

there are a lot of tools…Albert does woodworking

This seems to be a subconscious effort to shift the blame, or simply attention, to someone else. We know Letecia did blame Al. Point 140 on page 21 of the <u>Stauch Affidavit</u> refers to Letecia apparently struggling in her role as a stepmom, as well as being unhappily married. If she can't bring herself to explicitly blame Al, she can't resist implicating him – tacitly – in Gannon's injury. There is some truth, in my view, that Al is connected to what happened to Gannon, if only in a symbolic sense, because we know <u>Landen also accused Al of being an inattentive parent</u>.

Letecia's Facebook post continues:

*"He sat on the **edge of the car** and we **bandaged it up. He was good to go.** He always loves helping his dad in the garage build things like his LEGO tables and **the flower pot they built for me as a gift."**

Why would they bandage a bleeding wound in a dark, cold, dirty place like a garage?

edge of the car

Once again, Letecia's trying to create plausible deniability. There's blood on the car because that's where she sat coming to Gannon's aid. Inversions abound. Letecia is sneaky here not to mention a specific area of the vehicle [for example, where things are loaded]. An edge could be anywhere. This vagueness is intentional. Some things are being highlighted while others are selectively being withheld. That's gaslighting for you.

He was good to go.

This sounds awfully flippant under the circumstances. In fact, it sounds like the way a murderess might greenlight a premeditated plot, both the murder and the disposal:

He's in his bedroom, distracted by his game, he's good to go…

He's in the trunk of the Tiguan, body wrapped inside ~~bandages~~ a suit-case, he's good to go…

And then there's this:

the flower pot they built for me as a gift.

This and the impression of Gannon lovingly helping his dad wrong-ly conveys a situation of family cohesiveness. Just as in the Watts case, it's while one parent is temporarily out of town, in another state, and the other parent, the less committed parent has custody of the children, that the crime takes place. The crime happens while the family are frag-mented and also because the family has become fragmented.

"After this, I noticed G kept going to the side of the house. He told me he was checking to see if the gate was locked because he was the only one with a gate key. It made him **proud to be the man of the house while Albert was away.***"*

G?

Gannon is reduced to a letter.

kept going to the side of the house

Letecia may be responding to ADT evidence levelled at her by the cops. Perhaps she assumes the cops are reading this message too, and so its directed at them as well. It wasn't her running up and down the stairs covering up Gannon's death, it was Gannon running up and down the stairs.

"Fast forward, we did a hike on Sunday (cleared), and shopping on Monday (cleared as well for him getting out of the other side). Please **don't think for a second that there isn't enough of technology to deter-mine shadows and movement around the truck.***"*

Fast forward?

In an emergency situation where a child is missing time stands still. It doesn't "fast forward." We can imagine events unfolded at breakneck speed for Letecia though, as she tried to stay ahead of the curve. It's this speed, in a way, that probably did defeat the early investigation, along with initial inquiries. The speed at which Letecia hired new vehicles and appeared to cover up evidence, meant it took a while for the cops to realize there were really three vehicles they needed to pay attention to, and arguably, five.

don't think for a second that there isn't enough of technology to determine shadows and movement around the truck.

It sounds as if Letecia's talking about the Watts driveway, doesn't it? Shadows were a factor in that story leading folks to believe someone was alive when, possibly, they weren't. In the Stauch case it's the opposite – the absence of shadows led folks to believe Gannon was dead when it seems he wasn't.

Consider for a moment an extract from the above sentence in the context of someone that has hidden a body away, and hopes to get away with murder.

there isn't enough of technology to determine

Wasn't this Letecia's hope; that GPS and vehicle chips *couldn't* join the dots?

"There was also proof from my phone that we had taken a selfie in the truck in our driveway that was time stamped. We always send pictures to Albert when we are out and about or when he is away. That can be scanned for actual time verification. Last, from day one the Sheriff's office has known a description of the person/friend whom Gannon left with."

It's clear Letecia is overthinking every little detail, counter arguing this aspect and that issue, without being realistic, without seeing the bigger picture. Probably, she spent a lot of her life in that situation, and possibly that's how she ended up in the conundrum of being unhappily married, and then unhappily incarcerated. On the other hand, seeing the much bigger picture – the fairy tale – may be what drew her into a criminal psychology, like a moth to a flame.

The Particle-Board Breakthrough

"At the very moment when people underestimate you
is when you can make a breakthrough."
— Germany Kent

On February 14 – Valentine's Day – Letecia contacts her husband. She tells Al *four different versions* of what had happened to her, including that a wanted felon [Quincy Brown, not Eguardo] had car-jacked her, raped her, and anally raped Gannon. That's why Gannon's blood was on the scene.

In her latest fabrication, Letecia claimed she was with Gannon near County Line Road and Highway 105 [near Palmer Lake] in northern El Paso County on January 27th. She said Gannon was riding a bicycle, fell and hit his head. During this incident, Brown opportunistically abducted them both.

The description of Gannon having a head injury suggests he was likely stabbed or shot in the neck or face, in his bedroom.[49]

Page 27 of the Stauch Affidavit refers to "several interesting considerations" in terms of Letecia's latest whopper. The Quincy Brown Fiction transpired between February 12 and February 14, coinciding

---

49 The Stauch Affidavit points out at 165 on page 27 that Letecia's story lays the foundation for why "investigators may [discover] Gannon's body with head trauma."

with media coverage of searches covering the area between Highway 105 and the El Paso County line. According to the affidavit:

Letecia brought up this location on her own…and provided an alibi for why she was in the area. Letecia was adamant that investigator's efforts to search for Gannon in that area would be futile. This area turned out to be significant based on the Tiguan's location on January 28, 2020, and that **Gannon's blood was found in this area**. *[In addition], Letecia drove through this same area in [the] Nissan Altima…on January 31, 2020.*

Not discounting the fact that the GPS data allowed the search teams to vector in on evidence, it's still pretty amazing that any forensic evidence was found. It appears law enforcement were tipped off by Al himself, in terms of his conversation with Letecia on the 14th.

So it was the GPS data, the teams searching near the area as well as Letecia's paranoid response to it, that led searches to search the area even more intensely. This domino effect of data triggering more data and then triggering a response from Letecia, led directly to the particle-board discovery – finally – the very next day: February 15th, a Saturday.

One could argue that searchers had been in the area for three days, so if a discovery was waiting to be found, it was inevitable that it would be found. On the other hand, knowing that Letecia was getting antsy meant the frostbitten search teams could warm themselves with the knowledge that they weren't wasting their time; that something was out there waiting to be found, and sure enough, it was Gannon's blood on a piece of board.

According to point 171 in the affidavit:

On February 15, 2020, searchers located a piece of particle-board… The particle-board had a stain that appeared to be consistent with blood…The particle-board was collected by the FBI Evidence Response Team, and transported to the Metro Crime Lab [the same day].

The first test indicated the blood was human. A second DNA test followed. The DNA profile developed the next day, February 16th, matched the missing boy's. The blood evidence on the particle-board was the best evidence of foul play in three weeks of exhaustive searches, interrogation, analysis and investigation. It seemed the discovery of the 11-year-old was imminent. But two long weeks were to pass without any further discoveries.

Cat and Mouse with the Cops

*"I encourage you to think of any suspicious cars
that may have been in the area." — Letecia Stauch
Facebook Post, February 12th, 2020*

After the particle-board discovery, the investigation needed a break. Instead, nothing happened. The investigation petered out.

In the affidavit, the particle-board is described as an object Letecia used "during the disposal of Gannon's remains." Although the affidavit isn't explicit in its explanation, it suggests the particle-board was used as a sort of snow shovel.

Page 28 of the affidavit specifies:

The ground was covered by approximately six to twelve inches of snow.

It sounds as if Gannon's disposal was quick, clumsy and at the roadside. If that's the case, Gannon's remains would likely have been discovered as soon as the snow melted. So regardless of the searches, Letecia knew she'd have to find a better spot – and soon.

The affidavit also highlights the rural setting of the suspected disposal site. The weakest aspect of the investigation, in terms of the affidavit, is acknowledged here:

Gannon's remains have not been located…it's possible those remains have since been scattered [by wild animals, it's implied] since January 28, 2020.

Rural or not, America – and much of the natural world – isn't what it once was. Predators and scavengers no longer come out of the wood-work, least of all to feast on human bodies. A body entombed in snow wouldn't be easily removed by wild animals, and any effort to do so would leave clear animal tracks, and scarlet tissue traces, on the bright white snow.

Far more likely the monster that had hidden the boy's body had come to collect it, then hidden it somewhere else.

If we compare Letecia to Chris Watts *solely on the metric of how long it took to find human remains,* there's no contest. Letecia, certainly at this point in the cat and mouse game, seemed to have the authorities [and everyone else] stumped. On paper, and going purely by the numbers, Letecia seemed to be in the class of a criminal mastermind. Does that put Watts at the opposite end of the spectrum?[50]

The difficulty the El Paso Sheriff's Office faced in the search for Gannon was how big the picture needed to be in terms of the search grid. Typically you want to start with an extensive search, far and wide, and then start to exclude certain areas on your grid, and then narrow your search down. Gannon's blood on the particle-board mandated a more targeted search in mid-February. But what happens if, as you're narrowing your search down, an outside player who's scrutinizing your

---

50 If Letecia did a better job, in the criminal sense, of hiding Gannon's body than Watts did in disposing of his family, she did a far worse job in terms of executing the crime, or cleaning up the crime scene. Watts left virtually no evidence, and certainly no blood evidence, at 2825 Saratoga Trail. By comparison, Letecia left behind a bloodbath, and an orgy of digital evidence besides that.

tactics, secretly *interferes* with the game? What can happen, and what apparently did happen here, is that as the search narrowed, an action was undertaken that completely changed the game.

...there isn't enough of technology to determine...

What if technology could be used *against itself*? In other words, in the time it took to extract and analyze the data from Letecia's phone, and from the Tiguan's chip, what if the target was moved somewhere else? If that happened, then all the technology in the world was going to draw the search in to something that wasn't there.

In hindsight, it didn't taken a criminal mastermind to hide a body for as long as Gannon was hidden. Airport parking, a secret disposal under cover of darkness, piles of snow, a second disposal early on under cover of distance, as well as the use of valet service – none of that is rocket science.

In real time, from the other side of the equation, when investigators and searchers were still mired in the details, and mired in the unknown [including bogus tips], and not knowing the relevance of the Kia or the Jetta, it probably did feel like rocket science was required, and to some extent, it was.

~

"I'm Bleeding"

"We all have engaged in something crazy online at some point." — Letecia Stauch Facebook Post, February 12th, 2020

Do family dynamics have anything to do with why this 11-year-old was murdered? Well yes, they have *everything* to do with it.

It's thanks to Letecia's persistent use of social media, and addiction to her phone, that we're able to peek inside an encounter between the stepmother and Gannon – because Letecia herself <u>made and posted this recording on Facebook</u>.[51]

LETECIA: *Gannon, I promise this the last time I'm gonna ask you. I'm just freaked out, okay? A-Are you sure you didn't do it on purpose?*

GANNON [Tearful, overwrought]: *I didn't.*

LETECIA: *Okay.*

GANNON: *I did not…*

---

51 According to Paula Neal Mooney [AKA Plunder] Letecia subsequently posted the audio clip to prove Gannon was still alive on Sunday night. What she didn't anticipate was how bad she came off, and just how badly her dynamic with Gannon sounded, in the clip. In any event, Letecia used the recording to justify herself, even though what it actually achieved was the opposite.

LETECIA: *You promise.*

GANNON:*…do it on purpose.*

LETECIA: *You promise? Pinky promise.*

GANNON [Tearful]: *Pinky.*

LETECIA: *Alright, so…listen. Listen…we're…alright, we're gonna have to sell stuff to fix it, okay?*

GANNON [Voice trembling]: *Oka-ay.*

LETECIA: *We'll figure out what we gotta sell. We can sell the sofa. We can sell – whatever – cause we gotta get it fixed so the lady [Gannon sobs] don't be mad at us and kick us out the house. [Gannon sobs again.] Okay?*

GANNON [Gasps]: *Kay.*

LETECIA: *You got it?*

GANNON [Tearful acknowledgement.]: *Uhhhh…[inaudible].*

The timing of the clip is crucial – since it was recorded at around 21:00 on the day prior to the murder [January 26th], it very likely refers to the candle-burning-the-carpet incident. We know from Letecia's own Google searches that night, that *she simply couldn't let go* of what had happened.

I'm just freaked out, okay?

Besides the mini-narrative of the clip itself, there's a more obvious dynamic playing out. It's of a little boy who is clearly distressed, and his guardian showing absolutely no compassion. There's not a trace of sympathy in her voice, not a trace of acknowledgement in her words either, for his distress.

Her words drown his out. Even when he's answering she's already stepping onto him with the next coercive demand. Beyond Letecia's gripe with the boy, and the unhappiness with her marriage, it's fair to ask – what's the thing that's really eating at her?

On January 24th, a Friday, <u>Colorado's Academy District 20 rescinded their job offer to Letecia,</u>[52] who was due to start teaching at the Mountain Ridge Middle School. She'd already started her orientation, and parents had been alerted that Letecia was being added to the staff component. To their credit, officials at District 20 picked up "inconsistencies" in Letecia's application, and so, going into the weekend, she would have felt dismayed and devastated, anchorless and unemployed. And with Al out of town, who was there to take it out on?

In the same way that Chris Watts probably wouldn't have committed triple murder if he wasn't having an affair, would Letecia have murdered Gannon if she hadn't lost her job three days earlier? Would she even have been home, with excess time [and paranoid hysteria] on her mind, if she still had a job?

If Letecia's emotional resilience was threadbare by the end of the weekend, when the carpet burning incident occurred, there was also the underlying financial dilemma to deal with. The repair of the carpet reminded her that she was in a hole. In terms of her role in the marriage, she wanted out, but having lost her job, and perhaps future prospects of earning a living as an educator, according to her qualifications, this may have convinced her that there wasn't going to be an easy, or honest way out of the hole.

But there's a saying when you're in a hole:

"If you find yourself in a hole, stop digging." ⊠ Will Rogers

On January 26th, Letecia could have done with a few words of wisdom, because from this point onward, and at least throughout the

---

52 News of Letecia's unemployment status was revealed relatively late, on March 6th, 2020.

entire month of February, the 36-year-old dug herself a minefield of holes.

I'm just freaked out, okay?

Now, let's return to the audio clip and deal with the dynamics more in-depth. Without the context we now have, without hindsight, are the dynamics here of any real concern?

Ordinarily, we might be tempted to dismiss these dynamics as harmless. Because mothers and children might interact in much the same way on an ordinary day, especially if there's a naughty child and an exasperated mother, wouldn't they? But look closer. These aren't ordinary dynamics. The first clue is that **Letecia is recording the interaction.** In the middle of a crisis between child and parent, the parent is recording the interaction. That's already mighty fucked up. It suggests she wants to send it to someone, or use it in future, in order <u>to validate or defend her position.</u>

Letecia's interrogation of Gannon – because that's what this is – reveals that she's been hammering for some time, repeatedly accusing him of doing something [perhaps setting fire to the carpet] on purpose. When she says –

I promise this the last time I'm gonna ask you...

– she reveals she's trying to negotiate with him, so that he'll engage with her. She's agreeing that this is the last time, she won't push him any more on this subject, even though she has repeatedly accused him already. What she wants from Gannon, is *the recording of an honest answer.*

Given what we know about Letecia, her confrontational nature, her sly, sneaky approach, her bullying and manipulating of this child, demanding that he be honest with her <u>is more than a little hypocritical, wouldn't you say?</u>

I'm just freaked out, okay? A-Are you sure you didn't do it on purpose?

The clip is worth listening to a dozen or so times to get a handle on what's going on underneath the words. In sum, Letecia's accusing Gannon – while recording his answer – of <u>purposefully</u> doing something [we can safely assume the something that was burning was the carpet]. Was it done on purpose? Did Gannon burn the carpet to spite his mother? Or did he do it for a little fun? We don't know the answers to this, and can't know without getting to know the little boy. What we do know is Gannon was a neglected child, neglected by his biological mother,[53] neglected by his father, and over parented by his stepmother.

Although this may mean Gannon may have misbehaved at times, there's not a trace of pique, or cheek, or sniping at Letecia in this exchange. Instead he's completely submissive, and even though he's stung and hurt, perhaps even physically hurt, by the situation. He's compliant. He sounds genuine. He sounds sincerely sorry. Letecia, on the other hand, sounds like an ogre – heartless and mean.

Is he crying because of harsh words or because of something worse?

I'm just freaked out, okay?

Some have speculated that at the end of the clip Gannon weakly, and weepily says: "I'm bleeding." I'm not sure it's necessary to look into the vagaries of the audio for confirmation of what we already know. This seems to me is the Watts version of looking for ammunition for a particular theory in the shadows, only this time with sound.[54]

---

53 His biological mother was living in South Carolina at the time of the incident. His father was away on a business trip at the time of the incident. The fact that a stepparent felt overburdened with the job of parenting Gannon does suggest that his real parents weren't as present and involved as they ought to have been.

54 Plunder's "I'm Bleeding" video has been viewed over 150 000 times to date.

Instead, I think the tone of the speculation, of abuse and injury, is consistent with what Gannon was likely going through.

If Gannon wasn't bleeding at the time [and he may have been], I do think he was bleeding in another way – in the way that a child bleeds from the inside when they're not receiving the kind of care and attention from their own parents that they should. That bleeding likely went on for some time prior to the crime, and was Gannon Stauch's equivalent of Nut Gate. In the same way Nut Gate in the Watts case made Watts think he had indirect permission to kill the children [because they'd been symbolically excised out of the family before the incident], Gannon's Neglect with a capital N possibly made Letecia reason that if he disappeared, there wouldn't be much of a fuss. No one noticed him when he was around – except her – anyway. So would anyone really notice when he was no longer around? Would Al?

I do think the biological parents, though not guilty of a crime, aren't completely innocent in terms of the family dynamics. But we will address that aspect within the trial narrative.

What we know for sure from the audio clip, is that Letecia sounds less interested in Gannon's responses, or in having a conversation with him, than in superimposing herself onto the recording.

What Letecia does is manufacture a drama where **the expense of the damaged carpet is so serious, so critical, they're going to have to sell – whatever – or face possible eviction.** The drama itself is scarcely believable.

This psychology, this dynamic of overdramatizing an incident in a misleading way to gaslight her audience, provides a troubling precedent for what followed this exact moment a few hours later.

It shows:

1) *How the burnt Carpet Incident led to a **complete overreaction** in terms of triggering the murder [Letecia's crime is vastly disproportionate to Gannon's accident].*

2) *How Gannon's disappearance was initially **minimized, then overdramatized** as one rape/abduction whopper after another. [Gannon being asked to promise and pinky swear he's telling the trith, is vastly disproportionate to Letecia's lies and the scale and scope of her cover-ups over the next few days.]*

In other words, it exposes Letecia as a hypocrite bar none. Even on the Chris Watts scale of being a two face, Letecia's dramatic indignation stands out as extreme. But dramatic indignation is understating things.

What this shows is not only Letecia's tendency to exaggerate, but something beyond overstating, embroidering and embellishing. It's *paranoid hysteria*. Letecia at turns appears to be one [paranoid], the other [hysterical], and then a combination of the two.

In terms of the mini-narrative, Letecia sounds as if she's seriously asking a distressed child to help her raise money to pay to her landlady. No wonder she lost her teaching license! It sounds like she's asking an 11-year-old for suggestions on what they can pawn for cash. Gannon doesn't offer any suggestions. What's he supposed to do? He doesn't mention selling his television, or his Nintendo. Instead, Letecia appropriates his response by suggesting the sofa.

If we're going to address the narrow context of this audio clip within the wider context of what played out immediately after, and I think we should, we see that especially on the 28th and 30th, Letecia's hysteria over the cost of a damaged carpet was more than wiped out by her own *completely* unnecessary actions and expenses.

A-Are you sure you didn't do it on purpose?

Compare the cost of fixing a small piece of damaged carpet to Letecia's expenditures:

Firstly, hiring the Kia Rio. Secondly, hiring the Nissan Altima. Thirdly, parking the Tiguan overnight at Colorado Springs Airport. That alone would have set her back about $18. Fourthly, the price of having the Tiguan [and Gannon's blood] cleaned. Fifthly, Letecia had to purchase all the cleaning supplies required to clean Gannon's blood from his bedroom. Finally, what about the costs involved in his final disposal?

"I refuse to go look at a ditch or a pond"

"The last thing that they needed was a hindrance to their investigation." — Letecia Stauch Facebook Post, February 12th, 2020

On February 16th, the day after the discovery of the particle-board and three weeks since Gannon's disappearance, Letecia had a 40-minute conversation with a Facebook user. The Facebook user recorded the call, and then handed the recording over [apparently with Letecia's consent] to #Dadwithaphone who published it – as is – on YouTube.

Here's an extract.

LETECIA: *What did you say the question was again?*

FACEBOOK USER: *I mean honestly, did you say that out of spite, or out of jealousy, or do you honestly think she [Gannon's biological mother Landen] did something to him, or had someone do something to him, like, all the way from where she was [in South Carolina]? Like, was that really a thought you had?*

LETECIA: *Okay, so it's not [inaudible] all the way from where she was. Um, there was always like [inaudible] thing that happened like that in the past. It wasn't harm, it was the threat of doing harm on the children.*

So yes, I did think that, not because I thought she would have hurt him, by no means, that is completely not what I would have thought. But because I would have thought it make it look like [inaudible], or like we did something wrong. So that she could have him back. Because when moms are desperate, they do a lot of things, because they want their children.

FACEBOOK USER: *Exactly. And I get that.*

The Facebook User isn't an agent and isn't interrogating Letecia, that much is obvious. If it feels a little gratuitous [or even a lot], it's because it is. This is literally trying a case in the court of public opinion long before the trial. But it's a kangaroo court from both sides; it's not really an attempt to get the facts, or give them. The mere fact that you have a suspected murderer talking on the phone is online gold, the rest is secondary. The interviewer is acting on behalf of the social media mob, and the currency is gossip, as much as possible, and the more salacious the better. The more salacious the more likes, shares and chatter. It's like an <u>Ouroboros</u>, devouring itself.

One gets a troubling feeling of mixed up ethics here, not so? The one speaker's misdirections are clearly at a criminal level with huge stakes for herself, but isn't the person recording the conversation also more than a little mischievous in sort of going along with the whole thing? I'll pretend to be on your side, I'll sort of go along with your bullshit, in exchange you give me an audience, and I give you an audience. With my audience, I'll allow you to influence your own narrative even though I know [or should know] that it's probably not true.

If that's the game being played, what happens when someone comes along who has committed a crime, and manages to *successfully* implicate someone else, perhaps incite or manufacture a little <u>gang-stalking</u> while they're at it?

The reality is someone has murdered a child and hidden his body away. Pretending *everything is okay and I believe you*, under the circumstances of an imperilled, and as it turned out, dead child, is hardly okay. But let's be practical; social media exists, smartphones exist, and before criminals are brought to justice, they do sometimes engage with the media, or social media. It happens. So why not give them enough rope to hang themselves? I mean, how is this any different to Chris Watts' Sermon on the Porch?

Is it?

I would submit it is.

For criminals to become enmeshed directly in the social media fabric, perhaps even establishing a small network of friends, supporters and fans, what it does – what it can do – is it risks turning murderers into celebrities. We're seeing it already in true crime, where murder, or being associated with murder, can also make you famous. Book deals, documentaries, movies – it can be a ticket to the good life. Just look at Damien Echols and Amanda Knox. Not so much Casey Anthony and Stephen Avery. If you have mixed feelings about these names [and you shouldn't], that's the power of PR to make you see and feel differently. So allowing or giving the opportunity for murder suspects to participate in influencing their own narrative is like playing with a fire-breathing dragon. We should know better; we should do better than that.

When Letecia is asked to respond to **whether she thinks Gannon's mother is a valid suspect**, do the facts really matter, it's the fly-on-the-wall true crime soapie in realtime voyeurism that's in play. By merely fielding the accusation, however weakly, Letecia does succeed in throwing someone's name out there; someone's name who really shouldn't. Who, in the early stages of the loss of a child, deserves to be harassed less and supported more than the child's mother?

The fact that the video involves playing the audio while everyone watches a guy rolling his eyes – is that where true crime is going, or needs to go? If true crime is always and only voyeurism at someone else's expense, where someone else's trials and tribulation serve as a kind of modern day roman gladiators, with the colosseum replaced by Facebook walls and the number of retweets, what does that say about us and our society? Do we live, and enjoy living, at the expense of someone else's suffering. Are we entertainment by the blood, carnage and humiliating of lives lost and ruined, the more explicitly narrated the more entertaining it is?

If we're reminded of the value of life, and our perspective on life is renewed, if our compassion and love is awakened for our fellow man, rather than an a compulsive, voyeuristic fascinating with the villain, that's something. If we come closer to reality, and to stepping into the reality of our lives, that's a good result. But if we're simply using the wreckage of someone else's life to project our own superiority, express our own judgment on others, I'm not sure whether than edifies us or our society. It becomes a race to the bottom. And when you lie down with dogs, you get up with fleas. Lie down with liars and murderers long enough, you're likely to pick up the same problems, like lying, running away from reality, and blaming others, aren't you?

Besides the social media paraphernalia, let's be plain about what's happening. Letecia's not taking this call to implicate herself. It's the poor man's [poor woman's in this case] PR ploy – playing to social media. The media, like *CrimeOnline*, would [one hopes] give her a much harder time. Letecia's participating not to implicate herself, but someone – anyone – else. Shift blame. Move suspicion elsewhere. If she can implicate someone else, all the better. The Facebook User doesn't give herself a particularly high standard for fact checking.

Exactly. And I get that.

When Landen is slyly accused of having threatened to harm her own children "to make it look like "we" did something wrong", an accusation that's entirely false, the audience listening in get the fireworks, get their next episode in the ongoing tabloid narrative.

Elsewhere in the call, Letecia is asked whether Gannon was sex-trafficked. Letecia's also asked what she's been doing – has she been searching? Her answer to this question is worth taking note of.

LETECIA:…*I refuse to go look at **a ditch or a pond**. Not because I'm being insensitive. I just can't take my heart to go do that.*

FACEBOOK USER: *Who wants to?*

Despite the subject matter, and the length of the conversation, there's very little talk of emotion. There's very little evidence of emotion. There's not a single moment where Letecia sheds a tear or sounds as if she might be about to. All of it is matter-of-fact. But there is a moment where she herself acknowledges she's hurting, that's worth pausing over. Letecia talks about missing how things were at home "a month ago" when there were five people and two dogs at home.[55]

LETECIA: *Know that my heart is hurting. Know that – I-I might not sound like…this-this…but my mentality is always to think, next-step. Okay, I've already gotten over who woulda done this and why – because I've been in this mode for weeks, trying to figure out who I can punish, for doing this. And that is just how my brain went. So…now, I'm in the mode of being like…my husband, crying to me yesterday. Wants…I want my family back like it was a month ago. Five people and two dogs. In our home. And that hurts. And that hurts so bad. Because I'm sitting there*

---

55 Some sources suggest Letecia bought three dog coats [for two dogs] at the Petco on N Nevada Avenue <u>during two trips</u> on February 27th, and further, that <u>she didn't visit the Petco closest to her home</u>.

like…[Facebook User interrupts] so…the American Dream, you know. We made about $180 000 a year, together, we had a nice home. We had anything you could have wanted…Somebody don't just wake up and say, I'm throwing this shit out the door today.

Over a burnt carpet? No.

Letecia was hardly living the American Dream, but that's what she's selling. That her and Al, and two stepkids, and Harley and two dogs were seven peas in a pod. Letecia talks about an anniversary and going on a cruise. It sounds like she's pining for the past. But is she really, or is it just a *spiel*?

You don't understand how hard it is to be a step mom…[56]

When Gannon was alive she was fantasizing about him being out of the picture, but probably not thinking about how things would play out after that. From jobless, to getting rid of Gannon, and then going from being carless to homeless, and it was about to get worse than that. Fast forward three weeks – is she really pining for the way things were, wishing she could go back in time? Who was Googling about living somewhere else, finding a man with no children, getting a job in some other state? The life she'd left behind, including life with Gannon, was hardly what she thought of as the American Dream. And that's the point. This happened not because she was in a dream, but because *she was in a nightmare*. She wanted the nightmare to end. She wanted the fairy tale back. Gannon – she felt – stood in the way of all that. It was Gannon getting his fairy tale, or her getting hers.

The only way to get her fairy tale back was by passing on her personal nightmare, her holocaust of frustrations, to Gannon. Literally

------

56 Letecia sent the text about how hard it is being a step mom to investigators at 14:14 on January 29th, two days after Gannon's murder and a few hours after his roadside disposal. Source: <u>Stauch Affidavit</u>, page 20.

transacting her veil of tears onto him. By taking his life, she won hers back – that's the criminal psychology at work here.

So to claim her former life was perfect is misleading, but she wouldn't be the first. Many murderers lie about their perfect lives. Who would commit murder only to ruin the fairy tale? This is their alibi. Finding out that it wasn't a fairy tale after all, is how we also find out why the murder – for them – was an almost inevitable outcome.

The lack of a reality within the fabric of what leads to a crime, repeats itself in the conjuring of reality in its aftermath.

According to a post on _Medium_:

…Letecia had been obsessively posting on various social media sites. Instead of posting appeals to help find Gannon, she was professing her innocence and offering explanations as to what happened to Gannon, even **developing a timeline she posted on Facebook.**

What happened to…

REPORTER: _What did you see when you last saw him?_

LETECIA: _Well, I'm not allowed to talk about anything with the case._

But now Letecia's not just talking, she's conducting a parallel investigation, basically appraising a bloodthirsty social media crowd with supposedly exculpatory information in areas the cops and media couldn't touch.

On February 18th, <u>Letecia volunteered to take a polygraph at Fakepolygraph.com</u>. She provided them with the questions as well as with all the appropriate exculpatory answers. She was thinking – or overthinking – everything, wasn't she?

In late February, Letecia granted _CrimeOnline_ an exclusive. On the one-month anniversary of Gannon's disappearance, Letecia expressed her frustration at the investigation.

"They have spent all this time [searching and investigating] and haven't found him. Why? Because they are chasing me."

That statement has echoes of the JonBenét Ramsey case, and the Madeleine McCann case. It's basically yet another version of the ruse that the "real" suspects haven't been apprehended because the cops are investigating the "wrong" person.

Interestingly, in this anniversary interview, Letecia said Gannon definitely arrived back with her, because he was carrying a white bag. We'll get to the bag in a second. In another version, Letecia claimed it was ridiculous that she could have killed Gannon at home if video evidence never showed him coming back home – on the 27th. According to *CrimeOnline*:

Letecia said she didn't understand how authorities could call the home a crime scene after they saw Gannon leaving with her on January 27.

So she's playing the narrative both ways.

Now, in terms of the white bag, Letecia said she'd given it to Gannon in case he puked. According to *CrimeOnline*:

Letecia said the little boy "pooped in his pants" on Sunday, and had been having issues with his stomach.

Letecia was also asked to comment, in the exclusive, about the surveillance footage. She said:

"Something's not right…I never backed into the driveway [when we got back]." She said she did back the truck in the driveway that morning to let it "warm-up." Letecia added that Gannon dropped one of his electronics [likely his Nintendo] as he was getting into the truck, and she picked it up for him.

Bear in mind, Gannon was so ill, he was taken off school on Monday. Yet at no point did he go to a doctor, or did Letecia go to a pharmacy.

At the same time, Gannon spent most of the day not at home. The real mismatch to this story, is that when they returned home, suddenly, according to what she said to *CrimeOnline*:

***Gannon seemed to be feeling OK before he left for a friend's house.** He went down to his room in the basement area afterward, according to Stauch.*

Amazingly, after agreeing to the exclusive, Letecia contacted *CrimeOnline* to correct an error in their reporting. She was adamant that Gannon walked down to the basement after he arrived home, **but didn't leave through the basement door.** This emphasis seems to be aimed at the subtext Letecia had left with the cops – which was that she was raped and assaulted in the basement, and blacked out, and so when she came to, Gannon was gone [presumably abducted]. She didn't know how he had left, she didn't know how he had gone. This was why she wasn't a witness to where he went next, through which door, or in which vehicle. Convenient, eh?

CrimeOnline, to their credit, did a little detective work of their own, in terms of murkiness surrounding the basement, and Letecia's memory of it. They got hold of a copy of the ADT home alarm report from the Stauch home.

It showed activity in the basement and living room at the same time at around 3 p.m…Stauch said she and Gannon were the only ones home at the time, aside from their dogs, who were outside in the backyard.

When asked whether it was true she'd rented a car after Gannon disappeared, Letecia told *CrimeOnline*:

"The plan [in hiring a car] was to look for Gannon in a car he would not recognize."

This is a nifty rearrangement of the actual plan. The plan wasn't to look for Gannon in a car he wouldn't recognize. The plan was to prevent those looking for Gannon from seeing a vehicle – hers [the vehicle that had Gannon inside]. The plan was making sure her car wasn't recognized.

For the last weeks and days of February, it was starting to look like Gannon would never be found, and that the case was going to end up unsolved. The cops played into this narrative by not acknowledging what they actually thought. They knew, based on the large amount of blood evidence, including a saucer sized pool of blood in Gannon's bedroom, they had valid reasons to believe Gannon was dead. But they didn't say so. By suggesting he could still be alive, it played into Letecia's efforts to offer endless explanations for her behavior. No doubt, if the public were observing her statements on social media, so were the cops and the FBI.

According to *Medium*:

Letecia claimed she was being harassed online and should be offered an apology from everyone who suspected she could have ever hurt her stepson.

The cops also didn't immediately correct the speculation on social media and the media that Gannon had returned with Letecia on the afternoon of the 27th. This also allowed the heat to build online. Perhaps they hoped all this public pressure would get Letecia to crack. In the Ramsey case, a similar strategy was employed on Patsy, and in the McCann case, on Madeleine's mother Kate.

Arguably, when Letecia contacted Al on the 14th, to rant about the futility of the searches, *that was Letecia cracking*. While Letecia was trying to interfere with the investigation, and justifying herself, Gannon's family pleaded to the public for tips.

It was in late February, early March, that the cops finally let Al and Landen in on what they'd known for a lot longer than they'd been letting on. They didn't believe Gannon was alive. When the cops announced Letecia's arrest on March 2nd, Al and Landen continued to beg the public to come forward with information, only this time so they could give their little boy a proper burial.

Arrest

"I was constantly amazed by how many people talked me into arresting them." — Edward Conlon,
Blue Blood

On March 2nd, a Monday, 35 days after Gannon's disappearance, *Fox29* announced charges for the first time:

The stepmother of a missing 11-year-old Colorado boy was charged with his murder Monday and authorities are now looking for the boy's body...[But] reporters weren't told what led to Letecia's arrest.

But the coverage was misleading. Although the report implied the authorities were "now looking" for human remains, in fact, they'd been looking for Gannon's corpse for weeks, likely ever since they'd upgraded Gannon's status from missing to endangered on January 30th. Cadaver dogs, shovelling snow and remote-controlled submersibles all pointed to the same thing: the authorities suspected foul play. They weren't looking for an 11-year-old runaway; they were in pursuit and on the trail of a runaway stepmother instead.

Although El Paso County authorities issued an arrest warrant for Letecia Stauch on February 28th, Letecia was only apprehended two days, and almost 2000 miles, later.

According to a post on *Medium*:

El Paso County Sheriff's Office detectives, FBI agents, and members of the El Paso County 4th Judicial District Attorney's Office made the arrest of Letecia Stauch [in Myrtle Beach, <u>Horry County, South Carolina</u>] without incident.

Thousands of miles away, in Colorado, Gannon's parents, the District Attorney and assorted law enforcement made a contradictory claim: They didn't believe Gannon was alive even though they hadn't found his remains. The fact that law enforcement wouldn't say why they believed Gannon was dead suggested their case wasn't as strong as it needed to be. The arrest, on the other hand, indicated it had all gone on long enough, and what they had on Letecia was sufficient to meet the standard of probable cause.

When Sheriff Elder stepped behind the podium to address the media, the first thing he said basically gave away the self-imposed deadline the cops had set for themselves.

<u>ELDER</u>: *Thanks Jackie. [Sighs]. Um…welcome everybody. Today marks five weeks…since the investigation into the disappearance of Gannon Stauch. We're holding the press conference to update you on some significant developments. While we have yet to locate Gannon, this morning, just after eight 'o clock, AM East Coast Time, Letecia Stauch was taken into custody…*

Law enforcement have given Letecia five weeks' worth of rope to hang herself, and she'd done a fine job. They'd hoped she might reveal the location of Gannon's remains, or leak additional clues, but by the end of February, it was clear that what they had – especially from her side – was about as good as it was going to get.

It may also have been the strategy to offer a deal to Letecia. Tell us where Gannon's body is and you'll be spared the death penalty. In the Chris Watts case, the issue of the death penalty wasn't discussed in the media until the sentencing hearing. On August 21st, six days after Watts' arrest, when the Weld District Attorney was asked whether the Watts case was a death penalty case, Michael Rourke nonchalantly answered:

"Way too early to have that conversation."[57]

This was because the death penalty was very much a bargaining chip, or presented as one. To make sure the deal held, it was important that it didn't make it into the public domain. Had that happened, the potential arrangement would have been laughed at, ridiculed and shot down. The authorities wanted to avoid Watts [and his family] cottoning onto this early, pushing back, and the deal going up in smoke.

In the Stauch case the dynamic was the opposite. Because Letecia wasn't talking, why not let the world know prosecutors were "considering" the death penalty, even if it was never going to be a factor in the *actual* legal mechanism? As early as March 11th, barely a week after her arrest, the death penalty threat was making its rounds in the media. As far as we know, it was all water off a duck's back with Letecia. Letecia said nothing. Letecia dug in her heels.

The day after her arrest, Letecia – dressed in an orange jumpsuit, and wearing handcuffs – made her first court appearance. It lasted all of six-minutes. Ironically, Judge Clifford L. Welsh had something of sense of humor. His self-deprecating humor somehow made it seem the joke was all on her. It was, even if was a very bad joke.

JUDGE: *Do you know anything about extradition?*

LETECIA [Shakes head, croaks]: *No, sir.*

JUDGE: *Well, you're gonna learn.*

---

57 In fact, by about August 26th, less than two weeks after the incident, Watts' defense counsel were already suggesting a plea deal related to avoiding the death penalty.

When Letecia answered the next question, whether she wanted to fight extradition, she seemed to be lost in a legitimate fog.

LETECIA: *Um, sooo…when you said something about fighting it…I have to do what now?*

JUDGE: *So what do you want to do young lady? Do you want to waive extradition, or do you want to fight it?*

LETECIA: *So there's a hearing…what does that mean? If the hearing is here, what does that decide?*

JUDGE: *It just decides whether you go back to Colorado or not.*

LETECIA: *Well, I've still never been given the opportunity to, like, since the beginning to even call my attorney and even talk to him about any of these things.*

JUDGE: *Well, where's your attorney?*

LETECIA [Voice rises, eyebrows lift]: *Well, I have to call my friend Laura…*

Of course, when Letecia finally appeared in court with her legal counsel at her side, "he" turned out to be a she.[58]

In the final minute of her appearance, Judge Welsh explained that the only way Letecia could avoid being extradited was if she wasn't Letecia Stauch, or if the charges lodged against her were actually lodged against her by mistake, as in a case of mistaken identity. Of course in the very first sentence the judge, mispronouncing her name a few times, established from her that she was – and that her name was – Letecia Stauch. In his concluding remarks, the judge described her as a fugitive, adding, "I'm not going to set bond. With the charges involved, I couldn't set bond anyway."

---

58 Letecia's attorney at the time of writing is Kathryn Strobel.

LETECIA [Responding to the judge's remarks about being a fugitive]: *Yeah, I didn't run from anybody. So [garbled]…I didn't even know anything until yesterday. So the date you have on that paper is wrong.*

JUDGE [Setting her straight]: *Because of the charges involved, as far as today is concerned, I don't believe I'd say too much, okay?*

Letecia, for once, is at a loss for words.

Now, if we compare Chris Watts to Letecia solely on the metric of how long it took to make an arrest, Letecia seems to come out way ahead, right? But if one calculates the end result, and if it ends up being the same end result – life in prison without parole – does all the ado prior to the arrest really mean anything?

Chris Watts, compared to Gannon's stepmother, accepted his fate with some dignity, even if the charges against him were worse by a factor of three or four.

For Letecia the charges against her were:

First-degree murder of a child under 12 by a person in a position of trust

Child abuse resulting in death

Tampering with a deceased human body

Tampering with physical evidence

Joining the Dots

"The important thing is not to stop questioning. Curiosity has its own reason for existence. One cannot help but be in awe when he contemplates the mysteries of eternity, of life, of the marvellous structure of reality." — Albert Einstein, 2 May 1955, Life Magazine

The fact that Letecia needs to be driven thousands of miles, from Horry County, North Carolina, all the way back to El Paso County, Colorado, provides an important clue about Gannon's remains. Put simply, like Letecia herself, they weren't in Colorado Springs. Like Letecia herself, they weren't even in Colorado.

Three days after her first court appearance, while Letecia was on a 48 hour extradition journey by road inside <u>a white sheriff's transport van</u>, Letecia slipped out of her handcuffs and assaulted a deputy inside the van. The deputy was treated for unknown injuries in a Kansas hospital.

According to <u>*The Gazette*</u>:

Letecia spent a night in a Kansas jail before arriving in Colorado – her trip delayed by 12 hours – on Thursday morning, where she made her first court appearance.

Actually, this was Letecia's second court appearance, on March 9th. Unlike the prisoners seated on either side of her, Letecia was dressed in a black safety smock, typically used for prisoners on suicide watch, rather than a conventional orange jumpsuit. Letecia, through her counsel, indicated that she objected to all media coverage of her, and noted threats to her safety received through "threatening messages."

On the same day Letecia was formally charged with first degree murder,[59] Al filed for divorce.

Despite her objections, when Letecia appeared in court for the third time, three days later to face formal charges, the cameras were still rolling. Letecia, when she appeared, was in yet another change of attire, this time sporting a lime green jumpsuit. She appeared to hide behind her attorney when the camera zoomed in on her.

During the formality of dealing with the charges, it was established that 107 search warrants had been issued. We're not going to be dealing with this 20-minute hearing in this narrative. What we want to do is join the dots between the events as they played out in March, but also tie the strands across the rest of the timeline as well, between the end of January, early February and mid-March.

Before we resume with the timeline chronology, a few days beyond Letecia's third court appearance on March 12th, let's backtrack ten days to the press conference held on the day of her arrest. Specifically, let's revisit the emotional comments made by Gannon's mother and father. Let's start with Landen.

LANDEN: *I'm really not in the correct mindset to be standing up here, but if I had to be sayin' one thing. If he said Gannon is no longer*

---

59 The original first degree murder charge would later be amended to first degree murder with intent, and after deliberation, along with several other charges and counts added.

with us, I'd have to say <u>Gannon is with us…</u>Never thought I'd be standing here; it's a nightmare…Today I got the worst news, and the best news. Obviously we know what the worst news is. The best news is that justice will be served. [Sniffs]. And I will make sure [voice rises] that justice is served. Because my boy did not deserve any of this that has happened to him. So I urge media, one more time, just to hold off, of questions, till we know that this person, this person, [voice breaks] this stepmom that I even trusted, that she will pay [with emphasis] 100% for this heinous thing she done. I know where my son's at without a shadow of a doubt. I want to leave this earth knowing justice was served for my boy.

The difference between Gannon's mother's attitude to her son, and his stepmother's, is like chalk and cheese, isn't it? Landen is down-to-earth, warm, personable, tell-it-like-it-is. No frills, no phones, no fluff, no fanfare. No subtlety either. Landen is just plainly herself.

When the sheriff's office's spokesperson reads Al's statement, she too, chokes back tears.

<u>SPOKESPERSON</u>: *I'd been looking forward to his teenage years, and the fun we had ahead of us as he became a young man…[Long pause]. In a moment, on March 2nd 2020, my heart stopped again…My little boy is not coming home. We will never play Nintendo again. No more Taco Tuesdays. <u>No more smooth looking haircuts</u>. No more "Big Bubba" for my Lana. And no more G Man for the world. The person who committed this heinous horrible crime is* **the one that I gave more to than anyone else on this planet** *and that is a burden that I will carry with me for a very long time…*

Exactly two weeks later, and just four days after Letecia heard charges read out to her in court, sometime after 09:00 on March 17th, a Tuesday, a road crew in Florida are alerted to *something under <u>a long bridge</u>*. The terrain beside the U.S. Route 90 highway is rocky, downward sloping and treacherous. Upon <u>closer inspection</u>, behind <u>a green</u>

fringe of bushes, the crew discover a stained brown suitcase, and what appears to be the human remains of a boy.

"I refuse to go look at a ditch or a pond."

The remains in Florida aren't in ditch, or a pond, though they had once been when they were in Colorado, when they'd slept for four days under a blanket of snow. Five days after the discovery near Pace, Florida, the media announce the results of the autopsy.

~

New Charges

"It has been a challenge when people are trying to run you off the road." — Letecia Stauch Facebook Post, February 12th, 2020

Exactly 50 days after Gannon vanished, his remains reappear. As soon as they do, in fact as soon as the autopsy results positively identify the human remains as those of the 11-year-old, the full extent of Letecia's culpability, and cover-up in his murder is affirmed.

The remains of a Colorado 11-year-old last seen leaving his home with his stepmother – who has been charged with killing him – were found Tuesday in the Florida Panhandle, authorities said. – <u>Boston-25News.com</u>

By Friday, the El Paso County Deputy District Attorney, Michael Allen is addressing the media on new charges. Allen unambiguously describes the latest development in the Stauch case as something that "absolutely changes things…"

For starters, knowing for certain that Gannon is dead, and the extent of the effort to hide his remains, supports the idea of a deliberately violent murder in his bedroom, rather than an innocent accident.

<u>ALLEN</u>: *Today I filed, new, formal charges in the case against Letecia Stauch. Those charges are murder in the first degree, after deliberation, a class one felony that carries a potential prison sentence of life in prison*

~ 90 ~

without parole. In addition to that I've filed eight counts of crime of violence, for the alleged use of a firearm, a blunt instrument, a knife or other sharp object, and for causing the death of Gannon Stauch.

A few days later, media sites like *CrimeOnline* splash headlines like this:

Gannon Stauch, 11, allegedly shot, stabbed, bludgeoned, stuffed in suitcase & thrown off bridge by EVIL STEPMOTHER

Although it's difficult and dangerous to speculate, especially without the discovery, and given that so little information has been released, it is the purview of True Crime Rocket Science to put the puzzle pieces together, even with incomplete information.

Crucially, the autopsy results are not known at this stage. Nevertheless, True Crime Rocket Science suggests **it is unlikely Gannon was shot AND stabbed AND bludgeoned as some in the media and social media have assumed.** The above headline also misrepresents that Gannon was "thrown" off a bridge. More likely he was carried to a place underneath <u>the bridge in question</u>, and the suitcase <u>hidden behind local vegetation</u>. This would be an approximate match in terms of the effort the perpetrator went to <u>to get rid of Gannon in Colorado</u>. Instead of driving 35 miles under cover of darkness, this was a 1700 mile journey. Instead of burying Gannon <u>under a light covering of snow</u>, Gannon was disposed of almost as quickly, by simply discarding the brown suitcase below a highway and behind some bushes.

Some in the media have sensibly treated Allen's new charges with caution, like the *Denver Post*:

*The crimes-of-violence charges accuse Letecia of using **a gun, a knife and a blunt force instrument** in the boy's death, Michael Allen, senior deputy district attorney, said during a televised news conference. The district attorney's office **cannot elaborate on those charges, including***

saying whether she used all three weapons on the child, *Lee Richards, the district attorney's spokeswoman said.*

While there may be obvious forensic evidence proving that some or all of the above charges have substance, [and disproving the current TCRS hypothesis] in my view it's more likely there is a lack of evidence proving *all* of the contentions equally. The True Crime Rocket Science position is that Gannon was either shot or stabbed, or stabbed or bludgeoned, rather than a combination of these assaults. It may be that there is some combination of these assaults, but it's almost certainly not all. As a starting point, it seems particularly unlikely Gannon was shot, as will be explained in the final chapters.

One reason why more charges have been fielded as opposed to less, may be that the autopsy results **haven't revealed precise detail** in terms of a murder weapon, rather than what many have assumed – that they have. A clue to the reality on the ground, in terms of the state of the poor child's cadaver, comes from the use of two words referenced by the Medical Examiner, and repeated by media such as Boston25News. com

*"The El Paso County Sheriff's Office was contacted by the Santa Rosa County Sheriff's Office stating they responded to a call of a deceased juvenile male in Pace, Florida," El Paso, Colorado, officials said in a statement. "An autopsy was performed by the District One Medical Examiner and the deceased male has been **tentatively identified** as Gannon Stauch."*

Tentatively [a word that means "hesitantly", "cautiously" or "uncertainly"] suggests there was some difficulty identifying the remains. Quite likely the remains could only be identified by developing a DNA profile. Although we don't know when the remains came to be at the disposal site in Florida, what we do know is that the remains had been decomposing for 50 days, or close to two months.

In temperate climates a body can completely skeletonize in as little as three weeks. Since the construction crew were likely alerted to the remains by smell, it's assumed that the decomposition was incomplete, and ongoing. It is thus assumed that <u>the body was partially skeletonized</u>. This means contusions and cuts would be very difficult to establish, particularly where the flesh was rotten, discolored or eaten way. Only serious injuries causing bone fractures, or cuts onto the surface of the bone, would provide medical examiners with clues to the actual execution of the crime. The difficulty in establishing this would also have to be weighed against environment factors, such as impressions made by the teeth of predators, and post mortem mechanical damage, such as damage to bones based on objects placed on top of a suitcase, such as rocks.

There is also the crime scene, and Letecia's own statements to contemplate, when filling in the gaps, joining the dots, in terms of how Gannon was murdered. The most significant clues in this respect are:

1. The large volume of blood [indicating stabbing or bludgeoning].

2. The location of the crime [indicating the possible use of household objects or weapons kept in the home].

But perhaps the most significant clue is what's *not mentioned*. In its coverage, <u>*The Sun*</u> highlighted this hidden information as a pertinent point:

During a televised press conference on Friday, ***the attorney would not reveal what investigators believe happened to the little boy.***

It may be that the investigators haven't revealed what they believe happened, because just as in the Chris Watts case, they're not entirely sure what happened.

And, according to *People*:

A motive, if known, **has not been revealed.**

So what *did* happen?

So why *was* Gannon murdered?

Intertexualities of Time and Place

"Until Lee came forward, investigators testified they
had essentially no case against Frazee."
— *The Gazette, November 23rd, 2019*

Criminals learn from other criminals. Criminals who aren't criminals yet, are inspired by other criminals and other cases. Intertexualities of time and place, which is to say contextual elements, are what draws one criminal into the crimes of others.

The murder of Gannon Stauch shares unique intertextual idiosyncrasies with another high-profile Colorado case. What this means is Letecia Stauch likely found the psychological apparatus – the tools, the ideas, the wherewithal, the plan – from somewhere else. From someone else. From another crime at another time and another place.

<u>What was it?</u>

Going into Christmas and the New Year, something slowly woke Letecia inside her dream. Someone else's nightmare. <u>What was it?</u>

On January 27th, the day of Gannon's murder, Patrick Frazee, a rancher from Florissant who'd been sentenced to life in prison, announced <u>he was appealing his sentence.</u>

On January 28th, the day after Gannon's murder, Krystal Kenney, a former <u>Idaho nurse who was also Frazee's accessory, was sentenced to</u>

<u>three years in prison</u>. The Patrick Frazee trial[60] played out in late 2019, starting on October 28th and <u>concluding on November 19th</u>. If Letecia Stauch was influenced by the timing of any high-profile case, there was no candidate more current or more high-profile in Colorado, or in America, than the Frazee murder trial.

The standout feature of the Frazee case was that the authorities acknowledged that without his mistress Krystal Kenney's co-operation, they had almost no evidence, and no case against him. If the Frazee trial was a contemporary lesson in anything, it was how close Frazee came to getting away with murder. So, to be perfectly clear what we're talking about here: if you were thinking about committing murder, and wanted a quick lesson on how to get away with it, almost, the Frazee case was required reading.

We will deal with the unique circumstances of the Frazee case, and see how they match up with the murder of Gannon Stauch in a moment. Before we do, let's deal with intertextualities of place. <u>Are you sure you want to hear this?</u>

The distance from Colorado Springs to Florissant, Frazee's home, is less than the distance from Mandan Drive to where Gannon's remains were initially disposed of, in a ditch under a pile of snow next to the 105. Woodland Park, where Kelsey Berreth was bludgeoned to death, is even closer, less than 20 miles from Colorado Springs, and about the same distance – as the crow flies – to Palmer Lake.

Part of the fabric of the Frazee case spilled into Colorado Springs itself. Sean Frazee, who's the spitting image of his brother, is a Colorado Springs police officer. Sean saw his brother at his Florissant Ranch on Thanksgiving Day, the day Patrick Frazee murdered his fiancé, in fact

---

60 True Crime Rocket Science covered the Frazee case in *MURDER MOST FOUL*, and documented each day of the trial on YouTube.

immediately after the crime. Patrick Frazee also visited his brother at Five Guys, in Colorado Springs. During that meeting, police seized his brother's phone.

There's a Five Guys less than 15 miles from Mandan Drive.

In terms of the nomenclature, the Stauch's home is in the suburb of Lorson Ranch, adjacent to Jimmy Camp Creek. The Frazee Ranch and the trial in Cripple Creek have corresponding, if not similar semantics. Pikes Peak, and the fabric of tawny fields interspersed with rolling terrain covered in Pine forests, is essentially the same prominent geographical feature shared by both murder cases. The dark matt saw edge of pine plantations rising out of drifts of snow and dirt, forms the same jagged backdrop to the fate of the human remains in both murder cases.

In fact the fabric of the Frazee case and the Stauch are so close to another geographically, optically[61] and legally, they even share the same district attorney – <u>Dan May</u>. On February 5th, <u>Dan May was seen leaving the Stauch home with detectives</u>. On March 2nd, when Gannon was declared dead, and Letecia was arrested, <u>Dan May was one of the figureheads at the press conference</u>.

The same local and regional media personalities – reporters, <u>You-Tubers</u>, newspapers and news channels – have covered both cases. It's through the local coverage then, that a case like the Frazee case, and trial, would come onto Letecia's radar. For example, by appearing on

---

61 Patrick Frazee and Kelsey Berreth both owned red trucks. His was a <u>Ford Tacoma double cab</u>, hers a Chevrolet Silverado. A neighbor's <u>fuzzy surveillance footage also played a role in the Frazee case</u>. In the Stauch case Letecia and Gannon were seen leaving. But when they arrived back, the footage was less clear. Ironically, in the Frazee footage the situation was the opposite. Frazee, Kelsey and their daughter Kaylee were all clearly seen returning to, and entering the residence. It wasn't clear if or when anyone left.

local news bulletins, local street posters, as well as online alerts and social media chatter.

In her Sermon on the Verge, Letecia talks on camera about watching "a lot of law shows."

I pretty much have been told, at least ten different ways, that these people have these conspiracy theories. I guess they watch a lot of law shows.

Maybe Letecia did too.

<u>Now for the last.</u>

The Frazee trial, as mentioned earlier, was a contemporary lesson on how Frazee *almost* got away with murder. From a forensic perspective, the standout feature of the Frazee case was <u>the bloodbath left at the crime scene</u>, and the marathon cleaning operation that almost completely concealed it. Despite the use of cadaver dogs and an extensive forensic examination of the scene, the police weren't able to find much. It was only when Krystal Kenney walked CBI investigators through the crime scene, and pointed out *exactly* what happened and where, that they tore up the floor boards in the lounge, and found traces of Kelsey's blood where it had seeped through the floor boards.

Besides the crime scene, and unusual and unnecessary violence and brutality of the crime itself, the disposal of Kelsey's remains defeated investigators for weeks on end. Searches went on at various landfills, at the Frazee Ranch, and even in Idaho. Again, it was only once Kenney told them what happened, that they were able to figure out how Kelsey's remains were packaged, transported, transported again, and finally disposed of.

In the Stauch case, we see intertextualities in <u>the bloodiness of the crime scene</u>, as well as the bloodbath being rendered almost completely invisible. Like a pro, Letecia knew exactly what to do once the crime was complete: she sent Harley with a shopping list of essential cleaning items, much like Frazee issued instructions to Kenney [who cleaned up the scene].

A significant insight I learned while covering the Frazee trial and researching *MURDER MOST FOUL* was just how effective bleach is in destroying DNA, and also neutralizing the ability of cadaver dogs.

In the <u>*Argus Leader's* recap of the trial</u>, the near complete absence of DNA evidence was highlighted, along with how it was achieved:

Frazee's lawyer, Adam Steigerwald, said no DNA evidence tied to Lee was found at Berreth's home. Colorado Bureau of Investigation analyst Caitlin Rogers said that did not surprise her because the bleach that Lee said she used to clean up destroys DNA.

If Letecia learned from the Frazee case, if she used the fabric of that trial and the forensics to educate herself, it doesn't mean she knew how to apply it. A major difference between Letecia and Frazee, for example, is that Frazee never gave a single interview, and was a social media no-show.

The other aspect that's a signature feature to the Frazee case was the disposal of Kelsey's remains. Her bloodied, bludgeoned remains were transported in a black, plastic tote to a remote location, and then after a prescribed period [around a day or two] moved to the Frazee Ranch[62]

---

62 Kelsey's phone was transported 600 miles away, leading investigators to believe she was in Idaho, when she wasn't. Although "distance" is a similar feature, broadly, in the disposal surrounding the human remains in both the Frazee case and Stauch case, and for a time Gannon's remains were thought to be in one state, when they were in another, the **key weakness in the Frazee case** was that cell phone signals could be tracked. These signals clearly showed the movements not only of Kelsey's phone, but also Krystal Kenney and Patrick Frazee. If there was a lesson to be learned, it was to turn cell phones off and/or now allow them to be tracked. This is exactly what Letecia did when the crime was alleged to have taken place.

where it was incinerated. The irony is that <u>Kelsey's remains weren't hidden away</u>, but burnt in plain sight on a dirt road.

In the Stauch case Gannon's remains were also placed in a container, a brown suitcase, and transported to a remote location for temporary disposal. Since Letecia didn't own a ranch, she figured the only way to make the remains disappear wasn't through fire, but through distance, and perhaps water. Once again, if she had an idea and a plan, that was one thing, applying it [dumping the suitcase into a river, or the sea], wasn't as easy as it seemed on paper. And just as in the Frazee case, the remains weren't carefully hidden away, but disposed of using the substrate of a pair of highways.

Letecia saw herself sharing in many of the same circumstances as Frazee. Struggling to raise a child on her own. Struggling financially. Struggling in terms of employment. Also, her partner was often elsewhere, working, and that wasn't working out.

Although there has been some speculation that Letecia stood to gain from life insurance,[63] I don't buy it. This is an argument that almost never pans out in unsolved missing persons cases, because inheritance and insurance only pays out once a person is legally dead, and in missing persons cases, these legal milestones often take months, more frequently years to finalize.

In terms of motive, besides the symbolic and psychological aspects [which we deal with in the final chapter], Gannon wasn't murdered

---

63 <u>Insurance was also an issue that cropped up</u> as a potential motive in the Frazee case. According to the *Denver Post*:

After Kelsey went missing, Jennifer Barks [employed in human resources] looked at Kelsey's life insurance policy. Barks noticed that Kelsey didn't have a beneficiary listed. Frazee had been listed as her beneficiary previously...[In addition] **Kelsey was concerned about not having medical insurance for her daughter***...Ultimately, [it was decided] Kelsey's benefits would stay in place through the end of 2018.*

for a pay out, or for any specific financial gain. Instead, his absence, in Letecia's mind, would cause *less to be lost* – less of her time, less destruction of her property, less of his medical and nutritional needs to maintain, less of his life coming at the cost of hers.[64]

---

64 In terms of psychological intertextuality, there's something of a match here to Chris Watts, particularly the motives behind the murders of his unborn child and two daughters. Three children was just one to many, apparently, and one more Watts felt he couldn't afford. The Stauch home was also a three-children household. In terms of place intertextuality, Colorado Springs is less than 100 miles from Watts' home in Frederick, and 81 miles from Kessinger's former home in Northglenn. The disposal site near Palmer Lake is less than 60 miles from Kessinger's former home. To put these distances into perspective, the distance from Frederick to the well site near Roggen, where Watts disposed of his family, and back, is less than the distance from the Stauch disposal site and Kessinger's home in Northglenn. The visit to the Great Sand Dunes National Park by Watts and his mistress in late July 2018, took them right through Colorado Springs. On their way, driving on Ronald Reagan Highway, once they crossed under the Mesa Ridge Bridge, Nichol Kessinger's white Toyota 4Runner would have been less than 6 miles from the Stauch home in the brand new Colorado Springs suburb of Lorson Ranch. Besides that, the visuals of the new subdivisions, and individual ranch style homes rising in Frederick are a carbon copy of those subdivisions and homes rising in Lorson Ranch. In terms of time intertexuality, the Lifetime movie *Chris Watts: Confessions of a Killer* premiered on January 25th, 2020, two days prior to Gannon's murder, and the disappearance of his remains.

Boy, Interrupted

"Gannon, please come home soon because your daddy is waiting to watch the new Sonic movie that comes out this week and the cool shirt I got you to wear to the theatre is in your closet." — Letecia Stauch Facebook Post, February 12th, 2020

Restless, cloudy skies brood above the neat, buttoned up home, in the neat buttoned up suburb of Lorson Ranch in south-eastern Colorado Springs. At midmorning the mercury steams to its maximum for that day – 48°F [9°C] – before retreating again to below freezing. A restive, north-easterly breeze makes it feel colder than the frosty bite already in the air.

At exactly 09:56 on Monday morning, Letecia's fingernail taps against the brightly lit surface of her iPhone. The timing of the locking of the device is significant. Just as the phone is a lifeline reflecting the timeline of Letecia's life, it's extinguishing is a reflection of her commitment – at midmorning Monday – to extinguish a little boy's life too. It was important that Letecia's lifeline – its trajectory, its movements, its intent – not be fathomable from her phone. That act of leaving the phone at home, and leaving the phone alone, is symbolic of Letecia's departure from an aspect of herself [the mother, the caregiver, the wife].

19 minutes after locking her phone, <u>Letecia emerges on the moon grey driveway</u>. She walks swiftly toward the fire engine red Nissan Frontier parked in the road in front of the house. She walks around the front of the vehicle. She appears to be wearing a white, back-to-front baseball cap, or a beanie, and has a dark backpack slung over her shoulders. She gets into the driver-side, yanks the door closed, and soon after the vehicle pulls away. It arcs immediately into a sharp turn before backing up onto the driveway.[65]

From the backed-up position the rear cab of the double cab is just barely visible. The rear wheel is only partially visible. The vehicle is stopped in the driveway for 20 seconds before the door opens and Letecia slips out, moving briskly back to the front door. About 20 seconds later <u>Gannon appears</u>. It's very difficult to make him out in the low light. The red truck is a dark hulk behind him. Moments later two figures smudge over one another, and it's difficult to make out the one from the other. Gannon's dressed in a blue jacket, black jeans and sneakers.

At one point it appears something is dropped, and perhaps picked up off the dry, yellow grass. Perhaps its Gannon's Nintendo. A blue plume seems to illuminate in the cloud of inky smudges, and then another figure with something white on her head steps forward to open the driver side door. Just before a black vehicle approaches, Letecia gets into the truck. Once the black car has passed down the center of Mandan Drive, Letecia exits the vehicle again and returns to the house.

Nothing happens for 30 seconds. 20 more seconds pass. Now Letecia appears for the last time. She quickly slips behind the wheel of the truck. 20 seconds later, the truck shifts forward slightly, then stops

---

65 This manoeuvre is a carbon copy of what Chris Watts did prior to disposing of his family. The manoeuvre made it very difficult to see what was going on, and what was being loaded into his truck. The same scenario played out with the Nissan on January 27th.

again. Another 50 long seconds pass where nothing happens. Then, finally, at 14:19, the truck with its two unrelated passengers, draws slowly away and is gone.

Between the time Letecia locked her phone and the moment the Nissan Frontier exits the driveway, the ambient temperature drops 5°F [3°C], from 48 to 43°F [9 to 6°C]. The wind also switches direction, from 7 mph coming from the northeast, to 13 mph blowing in from the south-southeast.

INDIRECT CRIME SCENE

When Letecia was asked to account for her erratic movements on the 27th, Letecia told _CrimeOnline_:

...her whereabouts may seem confusing because she "took the back roads" that morning, "because there had been a wreck." [Then], at one point, she got lost and had to turn around. She also said she took exit 163, off of Highway 105, but did not remember the exact time.

What this suggests is that Letecia was scouting for a suitable killing site, and possibly a disposal site. Gannon being "sluggish" and basically incapacitated was important, firstly so that he wouldn't run away, and secondly so he couldn't put up much of a fight in a face-to-face assault.

When asked about Gannon's health, Letecia said:

[Gannon] stayed out school...because he was embarrassed that he might have an accident in class, since he was dealing with bouts of both constipation and diarrhea. Letecia said his medication[66] [sometimes] caused him to have stomach issues and bowel problems.

---

66 The medication – and Gannon's condition – has not been established to date. Some unsubstantiated rumors suggest that Letecia called a nurse on the 27th, wanting to know how much medication was "too much" for Gannon. This speculation opens the door for an accidental overdose scenario, as was suggested during the Casey Anthony trial. According to other unconfirmed

Gannon missed school, yet Letecia took him shopping, and when she needed him to have a miraculous recovery, he suddenly felt better and went to see a friend. The on-off nature of the sickness is a red flag, but that's not all.

It's not clear whether Letecia's intent during this four-hour period [10:00 to 14:00] was a botched attempt to kill Gannon, or an elaborate [but clumsy] attempt at misdirection, or both. The fact that her phone is off for the duration, indicates premeditation. There's a deliberate intent to cloud her movements, as well as Gannon's whereabouts, and likely other deliberations too. The fact that Letecia was in the far north of Colorado Springs with Gannon, close to a site she selected for the ultimate disposal of his remains, visiting a Petco 21 miles away, twice, and shopping for a bicycle without actually buying it, is suspicious. If she needed to go to Petco, why not go to the one off Cheyenne Mountain Boulevard, just 12 miles from Mandan Drive?

Clearly, Letecia's movements over a four hour period appear murky, and confusing, and Gannon is never *clearly seen* from the moment he gets into the truck to the moment he gets out.

From Letecia's fictional whoppers on Valentine's Day to Al, it does sound as if the criminal psychology may have been angled toward **driving over Gannon** somewhere around the northern outskirts of Colorado Springs, and then disposing of his remains.

Page 26 of the Stauch Affidavit confirm this psychology:

---

reports, Gannon had ADHD and was possibly prescribed Vyvanse. If Gannon suddenly **stopped taking Vyanse**, he would have experienced <u>severe tiredness</u>, but not diarrhea and vomiting. If he was deliberately **given an overdose of Vyanse**, he would have experienced confusion and disorientation, weakness, nausea, vomiting and severe insomnia. In <u>sufficiently high doses</u> Vyanse can lead to coma and death.

Quincy Brown followed her from Petco…[he] was laying in the middle of the road in front of her car [at one point]. Letecia stopped to avoid running the ~~boy~~ man over…

In Letecia's story, she spares the man's life, they then go home together and he rapes her in the basement. This is very likely what happened with Gannon, just replace the word man with boy, rape with murder, and Brown with Letecia and her use of a brown suitcase.

Had she executed the original plan, it may have been her intention to say that while she was away from home, Gannon left and went to visit a friend. This would explain her online searches very early that same morning, checking to see whether she would be culpable, as his guardian, for his care and safety.

School is out. **Is it okay for my kid to stay home alone.**

Son is sick *but I have to go to work.*

Son sick *can he stay home.*

Gannon's sickness may well be psychological code for him being sedated or poisoned. The neighbor described Gannon's final visible movements as lethargic. Indeed, while Letecia is running to and from her vehicle a couple of times, Gannon's movements are minimal, which is unusual for a hyperactive 11-year-old. When Letecia gets in and out of the vehicle, Gannon stays put. This is unusual for an 11-year-old isn't it?

According to *The Sun*:

[The neighbor said] Gannon could barely walk and looked "sluggish" in the footage as if he had been "drugged".

Since Gannon didn't go into Petco either, not the first time nor the second, it suggests he wasn't feeling 100%. The fact that he wasn't well, yet wasn't taken to a doctor, clearly indicates a high degree of premeditation from the very early hours of that Monday.

The use of the red truck may have been part of the original plot as well. It could be part of Letecia's misdirection too – to block both the appearance and the disappearance of the vehicle on the other side of it. In other words, Al's truck is sort of waved as a red flag to say – look here! Look to this vehicle in connection with Gannon's disappearance!

Bear in mind, later that afternoon, **the Volkswagen Tiguan had to be pulled into the garage in order for Gannon's body to be loaded into it**, and also, one of the vehicles need to be off the driveway for Laina to ride her bicycle on it when she arrived home at about 15:15.

Three obvious aspects that should be highlighted in terms of the timing of the crime:

1. The crime was committed on a Monday. Monday, as opposed to the weekend, or even Friday, was the one opportunity where Laina would be at school, Harley at work, and Al still away on his work trip. Monday was also a day when the neighborhood would decamp to work, meaning there'd be fewer witnesses. Monday was supposed to be a day Letecia would be at work. She texted Al late on Sunday night that she would take off work to look after Gannon because he was sick, knowing full well she had no work to go to [she'd been fired on Friday]. Her not informing Al that she was fired is also significant.[67]

2. In order to avoid raising alarm, Letecia let Gannon's school know ahead of time that he wouldn't be coming to class.[68]

---

67 Letecia not telling Al she'd been fired was psychologically similar to Watts not telling his wife he was having an affair, or not telling his mistress his wife was pregnant. There are sometimes severe economic costs to telling the truth.
68 Chris Watts did the same thing. Frazee also made sure Kelsey's boss knew wasn't coming into work. The point of these deceptions is simple: delay the raising of alarm, thus preventing the possibility of discovery.

3. Gannon suddenly developing a stomach illness is Letecia's version of Watts' "having an emotional conversation about a separation." In the Watts case, the emotional conversation likely didn't happen. That makes sense because Watts was an introvert, a coward, and confrontation wasn't his style. In the Stauch case, we know there was an emotional conversation about Gannon burning the carpet. That makes sense because we know Letecia's personality as an extrovert, as impulsive, obsessive compulsive, easily triggered and confrontational. Further, we know from her Google searches, that Letecia was still perturbed by the Carpet Incident – which happened no later than about 21:00 – for as long as four hours later.

In the end, the murder on Monday is hidden in plausible deniability and plain sight. Gannon is sick which explains why he's not visible, and not at school.

At some point, surely Letecia and Gannon have lunch. Since they return together fairly early in the afternoon, if Gannon was sedated to begin with, perhaps – while having lunch – he's sedated again.

All in all, it doesn't seem particularly sinister, does it? Letecia leaves in the morning, and returns in the afternoon; a very basic facsimile to someone with a real job, or someone caring for their own sick child.

Interestingly, in Chris Watts' fake story, he said Shan'ann was sick, and they were taking her to hospital. In reality of course, she was dead and he was taking her to her tomb. Same with Gannon.

DIRECT CRIME SCENE

The temperature in Colorado Springs recovers slightly, during the four hours when Gannon and his stepmother are out and about. During this period his life is literally hanging in the balance, depending on whether the red truck goes right or left, and whether random traffic appears on certain rural roads, or not.

Then, abruptly, the truck somewhere north of Colorado Springs, abandons its erratic movements hither and thither on backroads, between wrecked cars, wrecked lives and wrecked minds, and winds its way home. Now the weather warms, as if the beatific sun recognizes luck is on the boy's side. On the ground, crawling beneath overcast, moody skies, even the blustery wind pushing against the truck settles down suddenly, dropping from 13mph to 3mph.

Gannon is probably denied the use of, and access to his phone, while in the truck with his stepmother. When Letecia decides, for whatever reason, that murdering Gannon isn't going to work outdoors, in broad daylight [who knows, perhaps there was just too much traffic flowing along the 105 on Monday], she elects to use Gannon's phone since she can't use her own.

The appropriation of Gannon's phone also clearly shows intent. Thus *Can I play Zelda at least,* sent at 13:21, a response coming an hour and 15 minutes to his father's message, is likely not sent by Gannon, but is a kind of staged message to prove Gannon is still fine. Two minutes later, at 13:43, *can my parent find my cell phone.if its off* tells us exactly where the mind of Gannon's murderer is, half an hour before the little boy's life is brutally and permanently interrupted.

The Murder of Gannon Stauch

*Letecia said she planned to shop for **hockey equipment** for Gannon since it was the only sport he had shown interest in. — <u>CrimeOnline</u>*

[WARNING: THIS CHAPTER CONTAINS A GRAPHIC DESCRIPTION OF A CRIME SCENE].

When <u>the red truck reappears</u> on the overcast, moon grey <u>macadam</u> of Mandan Drive, it's 14:18. The truck could easily turn and park on the driveway, nose first. Instead, it pauses for a moment. According to Letecia, she took a selfie of herself and Gannon close to this time.

From *<u>The Sun</u>*:

...we had taken a selfie[69] in the truck in our driveway that was time stamped. We always send pictures to Albert when we are out and about or when he is away...

Perhaps at this point Letecia sternly instructs Gannon, once the truck is parked, to get out on the **left side of the truck** [on the side of

---

69 If such an image exists, it would be the last photo of Gannon while he was alive. According to the Stauch Affidavit, the last photos of Gannon were taken while he was in bed, asleep, between 08:13 a 08:17.

the Tiguan, facing away from the camera]. And perhaps she turns certain devices [like Gannon's phone] on, or off.

Then the vehicle pulls slowly forward, snakes slowly to the left, and backs onto the driveway, as before. The truck pulls fairly quickly on the driveway, causing it to bounce. After a moment, not satisfied, the truck lurches forward, then backs up as far as it can possibly go.

For about 40 seconds nothing seems to happen. Then the driver-side door opens and a figure emerges that doesn't quite resemble the one from four hours earlier; the one that was wearing the white headgear earlier, emerges. This figure appears to be wearing a dark hoodie. No one else seems to leave the truck, but apparently someone does on the side facing away from the camera. The Colorado day seems to hold its breath.

At 14:22 the ADT security sensor registers the opening of the front door. The murder of Gannon Stauch occurs now, in a relatively brief 23-minute window.

"Gannon, here's your Nintendo. You can play Zelda as long as you play in your room."[70]

The Nintendo game plays a significant role in Gannon's 11-year-old life. He gratefully accepts the game in his little hands, and heads down to the basement with his device. Letecia heads to the garage, opens the door, then backs the Tiguan in.[71]

---

70 If Letecia intended to murder Gannon, the safest place to do so in terms of eye and ear witnesses, was in the basement. Getting Gannon to volunteer to go to his room was theoretically easy: offer him the opportunity to do what he enjoyed most – gaming – as an incentive.

71 It remains unknown when exactly the Tiguan was pulled into the garage. If it wasn't pulled into the garage prior to the murder [and it's quite possible it wasn't], Letecia would **likely have had to change her bloodied clothes** before she went to collect the vehicle outside. In addition, if it wasn't pulled in before Laina arrived home, Gannon's body would have had to be stored somewhere else, before being transferred to the garage. While this could have taken place

In the garage she snatches one of Al's tools, possibly a hammer,[72]

---

while Laina was away with Harley, later in the afternoon, or after dark, it means some other place inside the home would have had to be set aside to store Gannon's body temporarily. The utility room, next door to Gannon's room, was available, but anywhere where Gannon's body was stored in side the house would then also need to be cleaned up. This makes it seem unlikely the body wasn't transferred from Gannon's room directly through the garage and into the Tiguan. Also bear in mind, in the footage, the Tiguan is directed with its nose towards the garage. According to page 6 of the Stauch Affidavit:

…the Volkswagen Tiguan…was <u>backed into the garage</u> when EPSO was at the residence.

From this description, it's unclear whether the Tiguan was found already backed into the garage, or whether it was backed into the garage while EPSO were at the residence. Given officers visited the Stauch residence about three hours after the 911 call, at about 22:09, it seems unlikely to be the latter.

Page 19 of the Stauch Affidavit is clearer:

[Sample] taken from the garage of the Stauch residence, directly under where the rear hatch of the Tiguan [would be] **when reversed into the garage.** *The DNA profile matches Gannon Stauch.*

72 The murder weapon – or weapons – at this point is/are unknown. It should be noted, a knife is a more plausible weapon than a gun. Filicide statistics from the *World Health Organization* [WHO] indicate <u>knives and blunt force trauma are the weapons of choice</u> between mother/son homicides in <u>over half of all cases</u>. An intuitive reason why a hammer might have been the preferred tool is because **Letecia implicates a construction worker** [though brandishing a gun] as one of her initial suspects. Construction workers typically carry hammers, screwdrivers, planks, nails and masonry equipment. Of these tools, the hammer seems the most logical choice for a murder weapon. It's also possible Letecia used a wooden plank or particle-board [perhaps even the same one with the blood stain found at the roadside near Palmer Lake]. Although the particle-board theory makes sense in that it connects to the garage, Gannon and Letecia, there's no indication that any tiny wood fragments or splinters were found in Gannon's bedroom, inside the brown suitcase, inside the Tiguan or in either of the disposal sites. If wooden fragments are found, it may indicate a board from the garage was used as a sort of wooden bat, or bludgeoning instrument. The reason a gun is assumed not to have been used is a) no bullet fragments were found at the crime scene

and heads quickly, quietly, downstairs to Gannon's room.

There are a lot of tools…Albert does woodworking…

She's a confrontational personality, sly and sneaky. She sneaks up on him now, her head hunched in cautious keenness, in predacious purpose. The angry frustration that's been building up inside her is so intense in this moment, she can taste it.

There he is…in his bedroom, distracted by his game. He's good to go…

She tastes salt in her mouth. Licks her lips in anticipation. Creeps a little closer. She has to catch him unawares, land a good blow so he doesn't cry out.

She takes a quick step forward and swings her arm. It's clumsy. The first impact is a glancing blow. The object makes a meaty thud against the top of Gannon's shoulder.[73] His body contorts mechanically with pain, a white gash opens, the precursor to the first fountain of blood. As the boy backs into the corner, trying to find his breath, or even a single word,[74] she lands the next blow. All he's able to say is a soft, "Nugghhh." There's a flailing of limbs now. He bounces off the wall, bounces towards her. She pushes him back.

He fell off his bike and hit his head.[75]

---

and b) no witnesses heard a gunshot. Again, this is an inference and does not definitively prove a gun wasn't or couldn't have been used.

73 The initial attack was to the head or torso, and his body was struck by a flat, blunt object:
*Gannon jumped on **Eguardo's back** but Eguardo was able to throw Gannon… across the room.*

74 No screams were heard by neighbors. This suggests Gannon wasn't stabbed, but lost consciousness relatively quickly.

75 In Letecia's scenario, the psychology of a boy riding a bike [playing on a machine], being distracted or caught unawares by some environmental factor, and then falling and hitting his head, corresponds to one of him

She sees the whites of his eyes, teeth, the mop of his brown hair bouncing. Orange blood splatters onto the wall. He has some fight in him. But inevitably a hard blow to his temple knocks him out.[76] She rains at least two, three more hard blows before she realizes the crumpled heap on the bed has stopped moving.

At once, her black eyes dart to the doorway, then to the window. She realizes she's breathing hard. She looks at the hammer, covered in a tangled stew of flesh and skin. Her hand is painted bright red, warm in the cold air, with the little boy's blood.

---

gaming [playing on a machine] and being attacked while being distracted. 76 In her various versions, Letecia claimed both she and Gannon hit their heads and blacked out. This reinforces the notion of a severe head or brain injury.

About the Author

Nick van der Leek *[@CrimeRocket on Twitter, @Nickvdleek on Instagram] is a widely published photojournalist and the author of over 90 books, including several trilogies dedicated to unravelling the world famous, and still officially unsolved JonBenét Ramsey and Madeleine McCann cases.*

Instead of journalism, Van der Leek studied law, economics and marketing. After two years cutting his teeth in a busy newsroom he became a full-time investigative writer. Today he is one of the most prolific true crime authors in the world.

He has sat in on many high-profile court cases and has occasionally advised criminal prosecutors during court cases on an extemporary basis. His research on the mysterious death of Vincent van Gogh has been added to the archives of the Van Gogh Library, in Nuenen, the Netherlands.

The next Rocket Science book, BOY, INTERRUPTED, THE MURDER TRIAL OF LETECIA STAUCH, *available in June 2020, focuses on the murder trial.*

For more superlative true crime coverage visit CrimeRocket.com, subscribe to True Crime Rocket Science on YouTube or become a True Crime Rocket Science patron on Patreon.